Ian M. Chapman

Do a Loving Thing

Judson Press® Valley Forge

DO A LOVING THING

Copyright © 1977
Judson Press, Valley Forge, PA 19481
Second Printing, 1979

Unless otherwise indicated, Bible quotations in this volume are in accordance with the Revised Standard Version of the Bible, copyrighted 1952 and 1971 by the Division of Christian Education of the National Council of the Churches of Christ in the United States of America, and are used by permission.

Other versions of the Bible quoted in this book are:

Good News for Modern Man, The New Testament and Psalms in Today's English Version. Copyright © American Bible Society, 1966, 1970, 1971.

The Bible: A New Translation by James Moffatt. Copyright 1954 by James Moffatt. Reprinted by permission of Harper & Row, Publishers, Inc.

The Holy Bible, King James Version.

The New Testament in Modern English, rev. ed. Copyright © J. B. Phillips 1972. Used by permission of The Macmillan Company and Geoffrey Bles, Ltd.

Library of Congress Cataloging in Publication Data

Chapman, Ian M.
  Do a loving thing.

  1. Bible. N.T. 1 Corinthians XIII—Meditations. 2. Love (Theology)—
Meditations. I. Title.
BS2675.4.C46   242'.4   76-48750
ISBN 0-8170-0717-2

The name JUDSON PRESS is registered as a trademark in the U.S. Patent Office.
Printed in the U.S.A. ⊕

CONTENTS

This book is a tribute to many people: to my wife, Jo, and children, Stephen and Stephanie, who have endured the pressures and trials of the pastorate with dignity and good humor; and to the Morgan Park Baptist Church of Chicago, who provided me with the privilege of being their pastor for nine years.

INTRODUCTION

In the motion picture *Oliver* there is a moving scene. Oliver, feeling rejected and very much alone, asks the poignant question: "Where is love?" Indeed, where is love? Love is that for which we seek. Intuitively we believe that if we can experience love, we will find our heart's desire and the fulfillment of our deepest needs.

But, what is this thing called love? Is it the stupendous, sensational feeling of ecstasy of which popular books and modern movies speak? Is it that feeling above all feelings which lies beyond description?

Love is always a mystery. Yet it is that mystery which tugs upon our hearts and motivates our lives. The following chapters are an attempt to understand love from a biblical and practical perspective. It is hoped that these messages from Paul's "love chapter," 1 Corinthians 13, will provide loving helps in our love pilgrimage through life.

Underlying these messages is a basic understanding of love. Frederick Speakman, a Presbyterian minister, gives us an understanding of love when in one of his books he relates this experience. In his first pastorate he struggled valiantly to minister effectively to the church. Often, the evening would find him with two elderly ladies. There, leaning back in a comfortable chair, before a roaring fire, he would pour out his heart as to his concerns and hopes for that church. In that church was a gentleman who used every opportunity to block every positive suggestion the young pastor made. One evening the pastor exploded, "How in heaven's name can we, as Christians, be expected to love a man like that!" One of the elderly ladies replied with wisdom: "You sound as if you expect to be fond of him. . . . Fondness . . . cannot be turned on and off like a faucet. Christian love is not fondness. It is not how you feel. *It is what you do!*"

Love then is not only that marvelous, moving feeling, but it is also a series of concrete and practical action steps which we take toward others. So that loving may become more real, a card that lists certain specific steps in relation to each chapter has been prepared which you may remove from the book and place where it will be a daily reminder to you—on the refrigerator, the night stand, the sun visor of the car. Use it daily until you feel you have made significant progress. These cards are found following page 16 and page 48 of the book. Each sheet of cards can be removed from the book and cut into individual cards as marked.

Let us turn then to the attributes of love as found in 1 Corinthians 13.

Chapter 1

THE
GIFT
OF
PATIENCE

1 Corinthians 13:4 **"Love is patient. . . ."**

The words of Paul are as contemporary now as they were then. Writing to the church at Corinth, a church torn asunder by controversy, paralyzed by contradictory views of morality, broken by partisan spirits, the Apostle proclaims the divine message: "Make love your aim" (1 Corinthians 14:1), for that is a "more excellent way" (1 Corinthians 12:31).

Surely we will not dispute his words! Love is the "more excellent way." Or as Dr. Karl Menninger once put it, "Love is the medicine for the sickness of the world." Dr. Menninger told his staff, including doctors, nurses, orderlies, and cleaning people, that the most important thing they could offer a patient was love. He said that if people could only learn to give and receive love, they would recover from their illnesses. These words contain not only the secret behind the amazing success of the Menninger Clinic in Topeka, Kansas, but also a truth we tend to believe. For love we will do anything. We will marry; we will divorce. We will make money; we will renounce all forms of wealth. We will stay at home; we will travel to the ends of the earth. Love is the driving force of our lives, the "more excellent way" of which the Apostle spoke.

But how are we to understand love? Love's definition is always vague and unclear. As the song of some years back asked, "What is this thing called love?", we are forced to admit we do not know. We experience love, we feel love. We need love, we seek love. But its meaning and definition is larger than that which can be contained by our words. When we turn to the Scriptures, we are given little help. Within the sacred pages love is not so much defined as it is described. In 1 Corinthians 13, the famous love chapter, the Apostle describes the wonders and values of love without defining his terms. Love is known only by its qualities and only by its behavior.

In 1 Corinthians 13 the first word used to describe love is patience. The question which must be raised is: why was patience listed first? Was that accidental or was there some divine reason for its position? Did the Holy Spirit have some eternal purpose in the placement of patience at the head of all love's attributes, or is it just a happenstance event? Personally, I cannot help but believe that Scripture is designed with deliberate intention. Patience is listed first because its presence is desperately needed within our lives.

We are such an impatient people! When William Pitt was asked what quality was most needed to fit a man to be prime minister of England, he replied, "Patience." He then was asked what quality stood second. "Patience," he answered. Pressed to say what quality came next, Pitt's reply was the same, "Patience." Having struggled with a stubborn Parliament, grappled with difficult international affairs, and sought to influence a complacent public, Pitt understood the necessity for a patient spirit. Most of us, I suspect, are short on this important commodity. The author of the book of Hebrews said: "You need to be patient, in order to do the will of God and receive what he promises" (Hebrews 10:36, TEV). We do have need of patience. Often we find ourselves behind a slowpoke driver. We are in a hurry. The hand falls on the steering wheel to honk our objection. The blood pressure rises; ugly phrases form on our lips. In anger we shout our impatience. Or, when we try to explain something to our children, they have difficulty understanding our words. We feel our impatience mounting. We snap a sharp retort and soon the child is in tears. How do we act when our husband won't clean out the basement or put up the storm windows? Or, when that teenage sister or brother takes too long in the bathroom? Or, on a more serious note, when we pray and it seems that heaven is silent and our prayers are unanswered? The illustrations could continue indefinitely, for the evidences of our impatience are many. There is obviously a great need for us to learn patience. Without that attribute we shall never learn to love.

One of the reasons we need to be patient is that God loves others just as he loves us. Among the treasures of Jewish folklore is this story. One day the patriarch Abraham saw an old man struggling up the hill to his home. Abraham ran to meet him and to help him up the hill into his house. He set a meal before him and asked the old man to offer the prayer of thanks. The old man asked, "To whom?" Abraham replied, "Why, to Jehovah, of course, the God and Father of us all!" The old man said, "Well, I don't know that God. I worship the god of fire." Outraged, Abraham threw the old man out of the house. But that night God came to Abraham in a dream and said, "Abraham, Abraham, I have put up with that old man for seventy years. Could you not stand him for one night?" Tragically, our response to that question is often "no." We find it extremely difficult to be patient with people, especially those who differ with us in matters of morality, religion, and politics. Show us a barefoot, long-haired, unwashed youth, and we will be irritable. Show us an aged, senile, drooling old man, and we will be grumpy. Show us, in fact, any person or group of persons who do not see things our way, and we will be faultfinding.

But, if we would hope to love, there must be a transformation of our vision so that we are able to see beyond the person as he or she acts to the person as he or she is in the sight of God! Can we cherish other people as the special and unique objects of God's love? If so, we can be patient with them! Can we uphold others as those created in the image of God and thereby sacred? If so, we can be patient with them. People are not machines, tools, objects, and instruments to be used, manipulated, and discarded at will. They are the solemn creations of God to be loved, revered, and respected. Once we hold people in that understanding, we can develop the gift of patience.

Another reason we must learn to be patient is that we never know the whole story. It was Alexander Pope who wrote: "Fools rush in where angels fear to tread." With these words he issued a warning that hasty judgments and quick decisions should never be made without having all the facts.

One of the most startling confessions of this human tendency comes from a well-known television performer. One night he was hosting the "Tonight Show." In the warm-up period preceding the program, he went into the audience, told a few jokes, and asked the people to applaud enthusiastically whenever they were asked. During the show the host introduced a guest and asked the audience to applaud. Everyone did so except one man sitting on the front row. He remained still and silent. The host felt his blood boiling. Seizing a microphone he left his chair, went to the front row, and thrust the microphone under the man's nose. He was about to say, "Didn't I ask you to applaud?" when he noticed that the man had no hands. It was a humiliating experience for the host and one with which we can, to some extent, identify. It reminds us of the prayer of the Sioux Indians, "O Great Spirit, help me not to criticize a man until first I have walked in his moccasins for two miles." That is good advice. We never know the whole story of the hurts, struggles, pains, burdens, and the limitations which dwell within the hearts of people. Since we can never know the whole story, we need to be patient.

Another reason to be patient is because we are not perfect. Thomas á Kempis, the devotional writer, speaks directly to our consciences when he says, "Endeavor to be always patient of the faults and imperfections of others, for thou has many faults and imperfections of thy own that require a reciprocation of forbearance. If thou art not able to make thyself that which thou wishest to be, how canst thou expect to mould another in conformity to thy will?" The same truth is expressed in the probing statement of our Lord when confronted by the crowd which had brought the woman taken in adultery. Jesus said, "Let him who is without sin among you be the first to throw a stone at her" (John 8:7). You will recall that the men, beginning with the oldest, perhaps because they had more of which to be guilty, threw down their stones and disappeared into the crowd. The point made by our Lord is painful and probing. Who among us has any right to be impatient when none of us is perfect? How can we be judgmental and superior when so often the faults we condemn are also in us? How can we stand aloof from others when in the sight of God we are all the same? Jesus once said, "Why do you see the speck that is in your brother's eye, but do not notice the log that is in your own eye?" (Matthew 7:3).

There once was a Christian man who used to say with Christian love, whenever he heard anyone being condemned or criticized for some fault, "Ah, yes, it seems very bad to me, because that's not my way of sinning." There is nothing more freeing than when a person has the courage to admit, "I, too, am a sinner." That simple statement is sufficient to save us from the sin of superiority and to enable us to be patient with the faults of others.

The fourth reason it is important for us to be patient is because God has been so patient with us. Have you ever pondered the patience of God? George Bernard Shaw once said, as he surveyed the evil and immorality within the world, that if he were God, he would send another flood, only this time there would be no survivors. Martin Luther said that if he were God, and people treated him the way they treated God, he would kick the world to pieces. But God is not like that. The truth of God, as we see it proclaimed within the glory of the Christian gospel, is that God never gives up on us. When we are disobedient and unfaithful, unloving and self-centered, God still loves us; God still is patient with us.

Some years ago a party of Arabs from French Morocco was taken on a tour of France to see the country. They were not overimpressed by the mechanical wonders of the bridges and cities and machines. But at the end of their tour they were taken high into the Alps by a guide. There, these men who had spent their lives in the dry deserts and barren mountains stood in speechless amazement before a mighty cataract which flowed out of the rock. When at last the guide said, "Come," they said, "Wait, we must see this." They filled their eyes with the wonderful sight. "Come," said the guide. But again they replied, "Wait." At last the guide urged them impatiently: "We must go before the darkness comes. What are you waiting for?" Slowly one of the Arabs spoke: "We are waiting for it to stop." "Stop!" exclaimed the guide, "why this has been going on for thousands of years, and will continue for countless years again. There is no end to this!" So it is with the patience of God. Even when rebuffed and rejected, there is no end to his love, there is no conclusion to his long-suffering, there is no writing of "finish" to his grace.

That, in the last analysis, is why it is so important for us to be patient with one another. If God our Father and his Son, Jesus Christ, have so patiently dealt with us, in spite of our disobedience and faithless living, how can we be impatient with others? Can we, who have received such mercy, be unmerciful? God our Father never gives up on us and we must never give up on others.

King Lear, in one of Shakespeare's plays, rashly banished Cordelia and Kent, the two who loved him, and yielded his power to the two daughters who despised him. He is enraged at his self-imposed powerlessness, and he cries out: "You heavens, give me that patience; patience I need!"

The words of King Lear might well be the prayer uttered by us all. Patience is what we all need. When we begin to see others as loved by God, when we pause before making hasty judgments, when we accept our own imperfections and acknowledge God's patience with ourselves, we are taking those positive steps which will help us to receive the gift of patience.

Chapter 2

KIND
OR THE
WRONG
KIND?

1 Corinthians 13:4 "**Love is . . . kind.**"

In Neil Simon's play, *Sweet Charity,* Charity is walking by a lake with her boyfriend. She is telling him how much she loves him, but it is obvious that her love is not reciprocated. In fact, he suddenly grabs her purse, pushes her into the lake, and flees. As she flounders in the water, a number of people pass by. A couple walk up and the woman says, "Look, Walter, there's a girl in there drowning." Walter replies, "Don't look, dear!" "But, Walter . . . ," she says. "Don't look, I tell you; don't get involved. It's none of our business," he says.

A football player comes by and calls: "Hey, there's a girl in there. I think she's drowning." About this time, an ice-cream vendor arrives and asks, "What's going on?" The woman says, "That attractive young girl is drowning." Another man comes upon the scene and asks, "What did she say?" The football player, now getting excited, says: "Jeez, I don't think she can even swim." And a woman says, "Sure doesn't look like it!" The first woman yells to the girl: "You should've taken swimming lessons! Now it's too late." A baseball player comes up and says, "Hey, I'll get my kid brother. He's never seen a drowning." And all this time the ice-cream vendor continues to hawk his wares: "Soda! Ice cold soda!" And he has another customer.

A man walks up with a dog on a leash. He asks, "What's going on? What's happened?" A man answers: "There's a girl in the lake. Looks like she's drowning." The man with the dog cries out: "Drowning? There's a girl drowning and you all just stand around? My God, why doesn't somebody do something?" And a woman indignantly says to him, "Why don't you?" And he answers haughtily, "I can't. I'm walking my dog."

What is love? The apostle Paul has told us that love is patient; it has a spirit of inner restraint. But love is more than patience. According to the Scriptures it is also kind. Love is a response of practical helpfulness which is to be offered to persons in need. If we would love, a diligent effort must be made to engage in that kind of behavior described by the apostle Paul in Ephesians: "Be kind . . . , tenderhearted, forgiving one another, as God in Christ forgave you" (Ephesians 4:32).

Years ago, Jacob Bright, a mill owner, was walking to his home when he encountered a poor farmer in serious trouble. The man's horse had broken a leg and had to be destroyed. People stood around the distraught farmer, telling him how sorry they were at his great loss. As soon as Jacob Bright took in the situation, he removed his hat, placed $5 in it, and said to the sympathetic bystanders: "I'm sorry $5 for our neighbor. How sorry are you?" He then passed the hat around and collected enough money for the man to buy another horse. Now that is kindness. It is the active, outward expression of love. It is a way of life which does not depend upon feelings or emotions as much as it depends on the awareness that the misery of life and the needs of persons require loving behavior and tender concern.

More specifically then, how can we love in kind ways? We need to learn to act without hesitation. Some years ago, I read a story in the *Reader's Digest* which literally changed my life. Written by a Harvard psychologist, William Moulton Marston, the article, entitled "Obey That Impulse," encouraged persons to obey the sudden impulses which thrust their way into their lives. This recommendation did not, of course, include involvement in that which was evil or tawdry. Rather, it was a firm declaration that a "do-it-now" attitude was one which led to great success. Once this psychologist and Walter B. Pitkin were retained by a motion picture studio in Hollywood. A young promoter presented an ambitious production plan. The plan appealed to both of them. Marston recommended that it was worth deep consideration, that they should discuss it, and decide later what to do. But Pitkin abruptly reached for the telephone and began dictating a telegram to a man on Wall Street. The message presented the idea with enthusiasm and conviction which resulted in a ten-million dollar underwriting of the project. Had there been delay to discuss the matter, the enthusiasm of the moment and also the project would have been lost.

Think of the life of Jesus in this regard. Time and time again Jesus was interrupted by persons in need. To the host whose wine supply had diminished, he could have turned a deaf ear. To the man with the withered hand, he could have given some excuse. When the woman expressed her love for him by anointing his head with perfume, he could have dismissed her action with flippancy. But, no! In each case Jesus seized the moment, grasped the opportunity, and obeyed the impulse for kindness. He provided the wine, healed the man, and protected the woman. He took advantage of life's interruptions to respond in kind and loving ways.

There is something valuable in that for us, isn't there? So often, our response to life is similar to that uttered by Governor Felix in the New Testament. Having heard the apostle Paul declare the richness of a life centered in Christ, the governor replied: "Go away for the present; when I have an opportunity I will summon you" (Acts 24:25). Or, to put it another way, "Later." How often we put off until tomorrow those acts of kindness and deeds of love which are needed now! There is a note of appreciation which is needed, but we will write it later. There is a word of love needed, but we will express it when it is a more suitable time. There is a need for an encouraging touch, a word of witness to our faith in Christ, but not now, the time is not right! Thus, the moment is lost, the impulse is squandered, and the kindness is not offered.

Perhaps it will help you, as it helps me, to hear the words of the Quaker governor of Pennsylvania, William Penn. He said: "I expect to pass through life but once. . . . If, therefore, there be any kindness I can show, or any good that I can do to my fellow-being, let me do it now, and not defer or neglect it, as I shall not pass this way again." "Let me do it now." How we need to obey those sudden impulses for kindness and love! The time is now. The present is all the time we have. We need to act without hesitation.

A second reason to be kind lies in our willingness to lose without regret. Last week I played one of the most frustrating games in American society. It's called "Parking Place," and the object of the game is to find a place to leave your car without two things happening: running out of gasoline or dying of old age. The game was played in the parking lot of a large suburban hospital. After cruising around the lot for what seemed like eternity, the telltale exhaust smoke signaled a departing car. As the car backed out, I edged closer. But as the car straightened and passed before me, another car shot around the corner and entered the empty space. I will confess to you that at that particular moment neither my thoughts nor my actions were loving or kind. I leaned on my horn, glared with anger and

1. DO A LOVING THING

Love Is—Patience

____I will thank God for his patience with me.

____I will seek to be more patient with my family this week.

____I will, by God's help, seek to be more understanding of people who irritate me.

_____

(signed)

----

2. DO A LOVING THING

Love Is—Kind

____Recognizing that kindness is the expression of patience, I will try to perform one act of kindness to another person each day this week.

____I will seek out a person with whom I have had disagreement (fight, argument, silence) and attempt a reconciliation through a loving act.

____I will thank God daily for his loving-kindness toward me.

_____

(signed)

3.   DO A LOVING THING

Love Is—Not Jealous

____I will remind myself daily how much God loves me.

____I will attempt this week to control my jealousy by seeking to love another.

____I will thank God daily for his gracious love toward me.

_____

(signed)

---

4.   DO A LOVING THING

Love Is—Not Boastful

____This week I will share one thing about myself with another.

____I will try to become more real than right in my relationships this week.

____I will seek to make myself open to the power of God which is available to me.

_____

(signed)

---

5.   DO A LOVING THING

Love Is—Not Arrogant

____This week, I will try to be a servant to others in the spirit of Christ.

____I will examine my actions to see how I treat people.

____I will consider another point of view that usually bothers me.

_____

(signed)

disgust, and began another round of the Parking Place game. Later I began to reflect on my experience in light of the meaning of kindness. Was it so important that I should get that space? I had to park several blocks away and walk ten minutes in the cold. Was that not more healthy for me? Besides, the parking place thief was an old man; he shouldn't be forced to walk so far in the cold. Not that kindness means, or even implies, passiveness or spineless behavior. Rather, there are some things more important in life than winning, such as compassion, tenderness, generosity, and love.

That point of view contradicts the values of contemporary American society. It is reported that Vince Lombardi, the legendary coach of the Green Bay Packers, once said, "Winning isn't important—winning is everything." That competitive spirit prevails within every segment of American society. It is found within the schools, the businesses, the family, and the church. It is, of course, one of the attributes which has made America great, but it has also tended to make America hard and coarse. The passion to win at any cost, to be successful at any price, has created immorality in high places and tended to blind the sensitivities of the American people to the hurts and needs of others.

Can we ever come to the place where we believe it is better to lose than to crush and destroy the spirit of another? Is it conceivable that the competitive spirit of American life can be tempered with love and kindness? Frankly, I don't know. We would be wise to hear the words of Napoleon, a man who desperately sought to win, but who was forced to lose. He said: "The more I study the world, the more I am convinced of the inability of brute force to create anything durable." That is a word needed within our world today.

Last, we can learn to be kind by being kinder than necessary. When Robert Louis Stevenson was a young man, he enjoyed recalling the most memorable night of his boyhood. "That night at twilight," he said, "as I stood in front of a window watching the darkness descend, an old-fashioned lamplighter made his way down the street, lighting lamp after lamp, and leaving behind him small pools of light. 'Look,' I called to my nurse who had come to take me to supper. 'Look, there goes a man punching holes in the darkness!'" Punching holes in the darkness of life is what the work of kindness seeks to do. By lighting the lamps of tender loving care, kindness seeks to remove the pockets of darkness which are so evident within the world.

In his book *The New Being,* Dr. Paul Tillich relates the moving story of Elsa Brandström, the beautiful daughter of the Swedish ambassador to Russia. Until she was twenty-four years old, her life was untouched by suffering or war. Then the First World War broke out. Within a few months, she saw prisoners of war being driven through the streets of St. Petersburg. Thousands of Germans marched by in the months that followed, herded like cattle, on their way to Siberia and to an imprisonment worse than death.

The sight moved her deeply. She decided to become a nurse. Then she requested permission to visit the prison camps. Wherever she could, she sought to ease the burdens of pain and suffering. She experienced the unspeakable horrors of war. Against these horrors, she pitted her love. She fought against the resistance of the authorities, the brutality and lawlessness of the prison guards, and the filthy, unsanitary conditions that bred disease. She brought food to those who were hungry, extended a cup of water to those who were thirsty, welcomed those who were strangers, and visited the sick and ministered to their needs. Her name to hundreds of thousands of prisoners was the "Angel of Siberia."

What will ever dispel the darkness of the world? Love, as it is expressed by an Elsa Brandström. Love, as it is revealed in kind and helpful ways. Love, as it is found in the Christ who taught his disciples to turn the other cheek, to walk the second mile, and to forgive in endless measure. Love, which is offered without counting the cost or seeking in return. Love, when it is offered without limitation or restriction, gives the world a chance of new hope and life.

Is that naive, idealistic, unreal? Perhaps. But has the way of the world succeeded? No, a thousand times no! The wisdom of the world has failed to eradicate poverty, crime, racism, and hunger. We are forced to the conclusion that the world, with all its pomp and power, has little hope except as love is expressed in kindly ways and offered in unlimited fashion.

There is within our world a Taboo on Tenderness. The image has been created that we are to be hardheaded and unfeeling as we live. But as one man has said, "If you are not kind, you are the wrong kind." And that is true. Kindness is the way of life which is desperately needed within this world, especially among those who would call Christ Lord and Savior. There is a need to act without hesitation, to lose without regret, and to be kinder than necessary for the sake of people. This way of life is beyond none of us. It costs no money; it takes no special talent or skill. It is within the grasp of all persons. So, let us be kind, rather than the wrong kind. Your God and your world are depending upon you.

Chapter 3

THE
GREEN-EYED
MONSTER

1 Corinthians 13:4 "**Love is not jealous.**"

One night when the desert winds blew hard and cold, a camel pushed his nose through the flaps of an Arab's tent and said, "Because it's cold out here, would you mind if I just kept my nose in your tent?" The Arab agreed and went back to sleep. Later in the evening he awoke and discovered the camel had not only his nose but also his head and shoulders in the tent. When the camel pleaded, the kindly Arab allowed the beast to put his forelegs into the tent, too. Then the camel said, "It's getting colder. Why not let me come entirely into your tent?" "Certainly," said the easygoing Arab, "Come on in." Before dawn the Arab awoke, stiff with cold and covered with the sand blown by the desert wind. He was outside the tent. The camel was comfortably inside.

The tragedy of jealousy lies in the way it takes over our lives. Little by little, step by step, jealousy spreads its disturbing presence to poison the heart and destroy the soul. Shakespeare called it "the green-eyed monster." John Dryden described it as "the jaundice of the soul." King Solomon left little to the imagination when he declared, "Love is as strong as death, jealousy as cruel as the grave." Jealousy. There is hardly anything in life which so thoroughly embitters the human spirit and poisons personal relationships.

The way jealousy destroys love is revealed within one of the first families. In the book of Genesis (37:4) it is reported: "But when his brothers saw that their father loved him [Joseph] more than all his brothers, they hated him, and could not speak peaceably to him." Or, see the way jealousy sets friend against friend. In the Gospel of Matthew (20:20-24) the mother of the sons of Zebedee asked that her two sons sit at the right and left hands of Jesus in his kingdom. When the remaining disciples heard this request, they were indignant. Why? They were hoping for the privileged positions themselves. Or, see the way that jealousy erupts into violence. At the beginning of the human story Cain, resentful and bitter that God would prefer his brother, let his anger rule his spirit, and soon Abel lay in a pool of blood, the object of jealous passion.

We hardly need, however, to go to the Bible to find illustrations of jealousy. We have only to look into our own hearts to see the role jealousy plays. Jealousy has been defined as "the pain successful people cause their neighbors," and we know that to be true. Have we not all felt the pangs of envy as we have looked upon the successes, accomplishments, and talents of another? Have we not all felt the fires of jealousy when one is promoted and we are passed over, when one is praised and we are not? Even within the family, jealousy raises its ugly head: the mother who manipulates her daughter so that she may not leave home, marry, and have a life of her own; the husband who controls his wife by his stingy handling of the checkbook; the wife who dominates her husband with her body. Yes, jealousy is very real. It is a bitter spirit which dominates and directs our lives.

The green-eyed monster of jealousy must be managed. But how? Well, it will do little good to denounce jealousy as a sin. We are all aware of that fact, and it will not necessarily change our behavior. Rather, we need to examine the causes of jealousy that we might attack the actual problem which is creating the monster's presence within our lives.

To be blunt, psychologists and psychiatrists tell us that jealousy finds its root in self-hatred and low self-esteem. Although possessiveness, checking up, controlling, and manipulating may have the appearance of love, they are less than that. They are instead declarations of the impotence and self-hatred which we feel within ourselves. Rollo May, in his book *Power and Innocence,* puts it this way: "The degree of threat a person feels at the possibility of losing the one he loves is the degree to which he feels jealous." Dr. Rochah, a psychiatrist, adds, "Jealousy results when love or self-esteem is threatened." There we have it. Jealousy, the green-eyed monster, raises its ugly head whenever unworthy, unloved feelings erupt within our lives.

The crucial question to be asked is, how can we manage these negative feelings and control the green-eyed monster?

We can begin by grasping the fact that God loves us. Once, a self-made businessman, who had just been named ambassador to a European country, came to see a minister. Most people would have been pleased with the honor of such an appointment, but self-doubt had convinced this man that he would never be able to master the social graces of diplomacy or learn a foreign language. In fact, he thought that he should back out of the whole thing. "Stop running yourself down," the minister told him. "Concentrate on the talents God did give you. You haven't been picked for your linguistic ability or your social graces. You've been picked because you're a tough, honest, plainspoken, patriotic American. That's what we need overseas. So tell yourself you can do a good job, ask God to help you, and go over there and do it!" Now, it may be difficult for us to identify with the task of the ambassador, but it isn't difficult to identify with his feelings of self-doubt and inadequacy. Time and time again we are confronted by challenges we cannot meet, relationships we cannot maintain, skills we cannot master, and feelings we cannot control. We do not feel good about ourselves and therein lies the crux of the problem.

How can we feel good about ourselves? A second-grader once wrote for his teacher an essay titled "My Face." He said, "My face has two brown eyes, it has a nose and two cheeks. And two ears and a mouth. I like my face. I'm glad that my face is just like it is. It is not bad, it is not good, but just right." How can we ever come to the point where we are able to look at ourselves and, like this seven-year-old, feel that we are all right? That question is of vital importance, especially in light of a penetrating comment from the columnist Sidney Harris. He said, "The only truth about child rearing that I am absolutely positive of is the fact that if a sufficient sense of self-worth is not instilled in the child at an early age, even a lifetime of continual success cannot obliterate that person's nagging secret sense of inadequacy." There is certainly truth in that sobering statement, but there is not the whole truth. As Jesus said, "I came that they may have life, and have it abundantly" (John 10:10). These words from Jesus contain the promise that new life and new power are available to flood our hearts and free our minds from all crippling passions. It is a promise which is founded upon a simple and yet profound truth— that in Jesus, God loves us just the way we are. In spite of our grumpy, irritable, nagging, faultfinding, self-hating ways, God loves and cherishes us. The other day I asked a car salesman what my old car was worth. He replied, "It's worth what someone is willing to pay for it!" What is the worth of a human being? Is it what someone's willing to pay for one? What is the worth of a person to God? The death of his

Son on the cross! That's how much God values a person! As Christians we believe we were created by God in the image of God and are therefore persons of sacred value. But the seal of God's love is revealed by the cross where God is declaring to humankind, "I love you like that!"

If we are truly loved and cherished to that extent, how can we maintain those ugly feelings of unworthiness and guilt, that nagging secret sense of inadequacy? In fact, is it not sin for us not to value ourselves as God does? A man of God once said, "Never build a case against yourself." These are wise words, for often we tell ourselves what we can't do, that we are inferior persons, lacking in ability, not capable of living life as it should be lived. But no more. We shall receive, into the depths of our being, the love, acceptance, and forgiveness of the God who has gone to such great lengths to show us how much he loves us. By his love, we shall build a case, not *against* ourselves, but *for* ourselves!

Another way to control the green-eyed monster is by moving away from an obsession with ourselves. When Jesus said, "Greater love has no man than this, that a man lay down his life for his friends" (John 15:13), he was striking a deathblow upon the sin of jealousy. Jealousy is selfish. It centers one's attention upon oneself. It is obsessed with self, what self wants, what self desires, and what self deserves. Christian love, however, is unselfish. It centers its attention not on getting but on giving. It reaches out beyond itself to enfold another in sacrificial love. As Rollo May states: "The more one develops his capacity for love, the less he is concerned about manipulating people and exerting power over them in other ways." There are two cardinal principles of love which are important in this regard.

First, the work of love is not to change people but to love them. There is a strange change mentality which seems to grip the minds and hearts of people. A vast amount of energy is expended in the attempt to make people the way we want them to be. But the task of love is not to change people but to love them, or at least to ask God to change us so we can love them. Look at the way Jesus dealt with people. He made friends with them, spent time with them, and regarded them with total love. What was the result? People changed. But they did not change in order to be loved. They changed because they were loved. Thus, we do not live to change people but to love people, and if we do, they will change.

The second principle of love is that at all times we need to seek that which will provide growth and fulfillment for persons. So often, our jealous mentality seeks to control and manipulate the lives of others. Unconsciously, we say, "I know what is best for you!" But do we? Is our concern for the other person, or is it for the betterment of our own lives? The question love would ask is this: "What is happening to the other person?" Is that person growing, developing, and finding fulfillment in life? Jesus said, "If the Son makes you free, you will be free indeed" (John 8:36). Does the other person have the freedom to try, to risk, and if necessary, fail, or are the boundaries too tightly controlled and contrived? There can hardly be a more important matter for our time. It would appear from the state of the church that ministers have not done well in setting the laity free to discern their gifts and fulfill their Christian calling. It would appear from the state of the family that husbands and wives have not done well in the task of setting their mates free to grow and find fulfillment. As parents, it would appear that we have not done well by our children, seeking their perfect behavior and their good grades before their personal development.

Out of the volumes of Lincoln lore comes this moving story. President Lincoln was a deep, sensitive man who often wept when he read the casualty lists resulting from the battles of the Civil War. Also, he seldom hesitated to pardon a guilty man if he had the opportunity to do so. Usually, the names of the condemned men were submitted to the president by their powerful friends: congressmen who represented the guilty soldier in Congress, high-ranking Cabinet members, or even the soldier's commanding officers. The president would note the high-ranking friend who was recommending clemency for the condemned man and quietly would write out a note of pardon. One day Mr. Lincoln came across the name of a man who was condemned to die. No powerful name had recommended clemency for him. "Has this man no friends?" the president asked, looking up quickly at his secretary. "No, Mr. President," the secretary replied. "No one." Quietly nodding, President Lincoln picked up his pen and, as he wrote a note of pardon, said, "Then I will be his friend." The need today is not for masters or manipulators. It is for friends—friends who care, friends who love, friends who reach out beyond themselves to set others free. May we be equal to the task.

There is an old fable of two eagles. One in his jealousy noticed that the other could outfly him; so he conspired with a hunter to shoot down the other eagle. The hunter replied that he would if the first eagle would only give him some feathers to put into his arrow. The eagle pulled one feather out of his wing. The arrow was shot but did not quite reach the eagle; he was flying too high. The envious eagle pulled out more feathers and continued to pull them out until he lost so many that he could not fly. The hunter then turned around and killed him. The fable helps us to see the tragedy of jealousy: If we do not manage the green-eyed monster, it will destroy us. So we have a choice: Give in to jealousy or give in to love. Which will it be?

Chapter 4

THE
EXPLOSIVE
POWER
OF THE
SPIRIT

1 Corinthians 13:4 "**Love is not . . . boastful.**"

Few people are so distasteful to us as those who boast. One day a man with such a reputation met an old friend. "I passed by your house today," declared the windbag. Whereupon the old friend replied, "Thank you very much." The boaster, the braggart, and the windbag turn us off. We would like nothing better than to dismiss them entirely, or at least, to cut them down to size. It was a hot, humid, summer day when a rather stout man went in search of his dog. He finally traced its whines and yelps to a no-longer-used conduit in the woods. The frightened animal could not or would not leave his hiding place. The man decided to go after his dog and forced his bulky body into the conduit. In so doing, he found himself so tightly wedged that he could move neither forward nor backward. He realized he could die in that pipe, and the thought of it terrified him. In this desperate predicament he began to think of his family, how selfishly he had treated them, how little time he had spent with his wife and children. The more he thought on that hot, sultry day, the more he worried; and the more he worried, the more he perspired. Finally, after hours of agony and perspiration, he lost so much weight that he was able to crawl out of the conduit a better and a smaller man than before! We might wish that we could keep a piece of conduit on hand for every windbag we meet! Nothing would give us greater pleasure than to reduce the size of each windbag perhaps while we recite the words of the apostle Paul, ". . . by the grace given to me I bid every one among you not to think of himself more highly than he ought to think . . ." (Romans 12:3).

The problem facing the braggarts, however, is not that they need to be brought down to size. Their dilemma is not inflated egos but punctured pride. The boasters do not recite their lists of victories, successes, exploits, and conquests because they feel so successful. It is, in fact, just the opposite. They feel such failures that they must seek every way to buoy themselves up. Thus, the braggarts are to be pitied, not persecuted. They have no need of the conduit, for they live in it constantly. They are little fishes in the big ocean of life who try to sound like whales, all the while hoping that no one will notice their minnow size!

Some time ago I met a retired businessman who showed all the signs of wealth and success. For many years he had run a successful contracting business on the West coast. Business had prospered; money had never been a problem. I shall never forget what happened one evening when a group of men were talking together. This businessman was telling, with obvious enjoyment, of the way he made his money. Whenever he finished a building and the city inspectors came to examine the project, there was never any difficulty. They knew that if poor workmanship and shoddy materials were overlooked, there would be a new car waiting for them at the end of the year! As the businessman boasted of his exploits and cleverness, the group was silent. One by one, excuses were made, and eventually he was left alone without the one thing he needed more than his money—a friend!

As Shakespeare put it: "The empty vessel makes the greatest sound." It is for this reason that the apostle Paul declares that love is not boastful. Boasting has a terrible, destructive, and strife-producing power. It disrupts relationships, erects horrible barriers, and destroys love. Therefore, boasting must be rooted out and eliminated from life. How can this be done?

First, we need to share ourselves with others. In John Powell's book *Why Am I Afraid to Tell You Who I Am?* there is a penetrating statement which probes my soul. He says: "If I tell you who I am, you may not like who I am, and it's all that I have." All of us can understand the fear that lies behind these words. On the one hand, we sense the longing within us to reach out to others that we might share our deepest thoughts and feelings. But, on the other hand, the risk of such vulnerability makes us fearful. Suppose we share those thoughts and feelings and we are rejected or ridiculed? Will we not be worse off than before?

The story is told of a Wall Street broker who met, fell in love with, and was frequently seen escorting about town a talented actress of stage and screen. The young man wanted to marry her but, being cautious, decided that, before he proposed marriage, he should have a private investigating agency check her background and present activities. After all, he reminded himself, he had a growing fortune and a reputation to protect. To safeguard his identity, he requested that the agency not disclose to their investigator who was requesting a report on the actress. In due time the investigator's report was sent to the broker. It said that the actress had an unblemished past, a spotless reputation, and her friends and associates were among the finest. "The only shadow," added the report, "is that currently she is often seen around town in the company of a young broker of dubious business practices and principles." It is never easy to face up to what we are. In fact, we will go to great lengths to protect ourselves against such pain. We will build walls of aloofness and erect barriers of busyness all for the sake of safety.

The other day I heard a radio commercial which intrigued me. The voice was that of a "hard-hat" type. It was rough, tough, and masculine. While I cannot recall the exact words, they went something like this: "I didn't know why people didn't love me. They stayed away from me. But then I began to open myself up to them and share my hurts and pains. And do you know what happened? People began to love me!" We must not miss the vital truth which is expressed within these words: When we take the risk of becoming vulnerable and accept the dare to be human, we open the doors to love. When we meet an all-sufficient person, who acts like a robot or computer, we cannot love that person. When we try to love a person who expresses no needs, hurts, or pains, it is well-nigh impossible. Unless there is a chink in one's armor of sufficiency through which one's humanity peeks, we feel separated, distant, and alone. Thus, if we wish to love, and be loved, we must become human. We must accept the risk of sharing ourselves.

One of the loveliest stories is called "The Velveteen Rabbit." "In this story a little velveteen rabbit is loved by a small boy. It was once new and shiny on Christmas morning, and it lived in the nursery and talked to the other toys. The mechanical toys felt especially superior and pretended they were real because they had springs and could move. The Rabbit asked the Skin Horse, who was the oldest and wisest toy: 'What is Real? Does it mean having things that buzz inside you and a stick-out handle?' 'Real isn't how you are made,' said the Horse. 'It's a thing that happens to you. When a child loves you for a long, long time, then you become Real.' 'Does it hurt?' asked the Rabbit. 'Sometimes,' said the Horse. 'But when you are Real, you don't mind being hurt.' 'Does it happen all at once, like being wound up, or bit-by-bit?' 'It doesn't happen all-at-once,' said the Horse. 'You become. It takes a long time. That's why it doesn't happen often to people who break easily, or have sharp edges, or who have to be carefully kept. Generally, by the time you are Real, most of your hair has been loved off, and your eyes drop out, and you get loose in the joints, and very shabby. But these things don't matter at all, because, once you are Real, you can't be ugly, except to people who don't understand.'" So the Velveteen Rabbit was loved by the boy, dragged around the garden, and left out in the dew so that he became very shabby. One day the nurse tried to throw him away, and the boy said, "You can't do that. He isn't a toy; he's Real!" And the rabbit shivered with joy, for he realized that the nursery magic had happened to him. At last he was real!

To be real—that is more important than being right. To be right is to keep the world at arm's distance, while boasting of victories and accomplishments. It is to be a toy-person, mechanical, and cold. Whereas, to be real is to be able to say, "I'm me. I have faults. I have weaknesses. I make mistakes. I do dumb things. But I'm going to share myself with you that we might learn to love one another." It is in that sharing that boasting is finally beaten.

To offset our natural inclination to boast, we need to seize the power of God. One of the stories which always means a great deal to me comes from the life of Alexander MacLaren, the Scottish preacher. When he was just a young lad, he left school to begin work. His job was in the next village some miles away. His father said, "Now, Alex, this is the first time that you will have been away from home. When Friday comes, I want you to come home right after work." Alex started to disagree, for between the two villages lay a deep and dark ravine which in Alex's childish imagination had always been filled with ghosts and goblins. But he agreed and went off to work. When Friday came, he started the journey home. He was frightened but was determined not to show it. Just as he came to the ravine, a storm struck. The thunder rolled, the lightning flashed across the sky. Alex walked faster. His mouth was dry and his heart was pounding. Just then he heard the sound of steps coming toward him. His heart rose up into his mouth and as he turned to flee, a familiar voice came out of the darkness, "Alex, it's me, your father. I knew you would be traveling in the dark, and I came to meet you." With that he put his arm around the boy's shoulder, and together they walked through the storm. Now it is important to say that God is not a lucky charm whose presence automatically protects against all harm and evil. It is, however, important to say that the presence of

God is that vital ingredient which has the power to meet us in our times of darkness and bewilderment to reshape and remold our lives.

One of the cardinal Christian truths is that whenever we place our faith in Jesus Christ and commit ourselves to him, the Holy Spirit comes to live within us. God is no distant creator or abstract deity. He is in the Holy Spirit, our ever-present Companion and eternal Contemporary. It is important for a moment that we think together of this Holy Spirit. What does it mean for us that he should live within our hearts? More than we could ever realize. In the book of Acts we read of the miracle of Pentecost. The Holy Spirit descended upon the disciples, filling them with power and sending them forth into the streets to proclaim the resurrection message of the Christ. The disciples, it is reported, had been cowering in fear behind locked doors in the upper room. They became bold, courageous, and brazen witnesses for Christ. What could have prompted such a miracle? The answer is found in the Holy Spirit. In the New Testament, the Holy Spirit means power. The Scripture declares, "But you shall receive power when the Holy Spirit has come upon you . . ." (Acts 1:8). That word "power" in the Greek is the word from which we derive our word "dynamite." Thus, the Holy Spirit brings to every Christian person a power which has the explosive force of dynamite.

This discourse on the Holy Spirit may seem a long detour from a discussion on boasting, but it is connected. For rather than boasting in an effort to cover up the powerlessness and inadequacy of our empty lives, we need to seize the explosive power of the Holy Spirit which is already within us! We need not brag, boast, conquer, and manipulate to seek more effective living. We need only to make ourselves receptive to the powerful presence of the Holy Spirit that is already within us that he might make us into effective instruments of his love. Think of what that can do for our lives, our homes, our churches, and our world! The explosive power of God is within us right now. We need not fear, cower, conceal, or fuss. And when that power permeates our lives, there is no reason to boast except of the God who meets us at our point of deepest need and rescues us from ourselves.

Someone once said, "The trouble with singing your own praises is that you seldom get the right pitch." Truer words have rarely been spoken. The boasting, bragging spirit is perhaps the emptiest, most futile exercise for our lives. Rather, we need to share ourselves with others that, through the explosive power of the Spirit, we might become new. Wouldn't that bring great joy?

Chapter 5

CHARLIE AND THE JEHOVAH COMPLEX

1 Corinthians 13:5 "**Love is** . . . **not arrogant**"

One day a minister went to see Charlie. Charlie was recovering from a recent operation, and it was obvious that he was fretting, not about his physical condition which was excellent, but because he had to remain idle in the hospital. When the minister asked how he was, his wife answered for him. Smiling, she said, "Fine, except that he suffers from a Jehovah complex." The minister looked startled. The wife explained: "My husband suffers from the illusion that he is the Almighty, or at least his general manager! He feels that the world won't turn properly unless he's back in his office, or presiding over a committee meeting, or seeing the right people!"

We may not all act just that way, but the Jehovah complex is not Charlie's problem alone. Think of the number of times we put things off—that doctor's visit, that work around the house, that overdue vacation, that family responsibility. Why? At heart we cannot bear to be separated from our duties for even a moment. The Jehovah complex creates a Messiah mentality within us. We, and we alone, can save the world. Without us the world will be much the poorer and things just can't go right.

The story is told of a slightly over-rouged young lady who summoned the headwaiter: "That's Paul Newman over at the bar, isn't it?" she asked. He assured her that it was. "He's annoying me," she said. "Annoying you?" the headwaiter asked as he raised an eyebrow. "Why, he hasn't even looked at you!" "That," said the young lady, "is what's annoying me." That is the fear which lies behind the Jehovah complex. We hate to think that we could be overlooked in life and left out. Such a thought is too terrible for our weak egos to imagine.

The trouble with such a spirit lies in the temptation to think more highly of ourselves than we ought to think and to act in a haughty and superior way. Jesus once told a story which illustrates that tendency. Two men went up into the temple to pray. The tax collector, so humble that he could not even lift his head to heaven, prayed, "God, be merciful to me a sinner!" The Pharisee waddled up into the presence of God and prayed: "God, I thank thee that I am not like other men, extortioners, unjust, adulterers, or even [and here you sense that he casts a disparaging look upon the tax collector] like this tax collector. I fast twice a week, I give tithes of all that I get" (see Luke 18:10-14). Which of these two men would you prefer for your friend? The choice is obvious, isn't it? The Pharisee with his peacock spirit, his Jehovah complex, turns us off. We do not feel comfortable in the presence of such a self-righteous prig. His arrogance is offensive.

How can we deal with such a destructive spirit? First, we can remind ourselves of the words of Paul—that love is not arrogant. Then, we can carefully ask ourselves some pointed questions to determine the place arrogance holds within our hearts. Such a question is:

Am I teachable?

There is a story of a politician who was told by a minister that if he stood outside, looking up into the heavens, he would receive a special revelation. The politician, eager to try anything, did as the minister suggested. Later, however, he reported his disappointment. "When I looked up into the heavens," he said, "it started to rain. The water ran down my neck and I felt like a fool." "Well," the minister said, "that's quite a revelation, isn't it?" Most persons, however, are not too interested in such new revelations. They are more interested in maintaining their point of view, tightening their handles on their truth, and protecting their understanding of reality.

The core of the problem is this: How can the Christian be certain about his or her faith but not arrogant? How can the Christian claim that Jesus Christ is "the way, the truth, and the life," "the name under heaven by which all men must be saved" and at the same time be loving and accepting of others? The church throughout the centuries has not dealt wisely with that issue. As a result, the world is filled with rebels who have left the church reacting against a narrow, limited, and parochial view of truth expressed by the church.

The fact of the situation, especially made clear in this fast-changing, future-shock world of ours, is that all the truth is not known to us, not even to the church. You will recall the famous story about a group of blind men who were given the task of describing an elephant. Each man felt a different part of the elephant and then announced his description of the beast. But the men were unable to see the whole elephant. Their understanding was distorted and partial. This is what Paul meant when he wrote in 1 Corinthians 13:12; "Now we see through a glass darkly." All the facts are not known; the evidence is not complete. As humans we are not able to see enough of the data to be dogmatic and certain. A cartoon appeared in a New York paper one June at the time of the college commencements. It pictured a young woman in cap and gown, armed with her college diploma and a sufficient amount of self-satisfied dignity. Confronting her was the grim face of the world, old and wizened, who remarked rather casually, "Well, who have we here?" "You don't know me?" replied the disappointed graduate. "I am Virginia Cordelia Smith, A.B." "My dear girl," replied the world, "come with me and I will teach you the rest of your alphabet!"

As Christians it is important for us to understand that we have much to learn and that a spirit of openness must characterize our life-styles. By this, I do not mean an empty-headedness where there is no warmth of conviction about the things that truly matter, but an openness to truth as it is centered in Christ and the Scriptures, and a receptivity to truth as it is contained elsewhere in the world. An open-minded person refuses to say, "I have arrived, I have the truth." Instead, he cries with the apostle Paul, "I press on. . . ."

The implications of such an open stance are exciting. It suggests that the old will no longer dismiss the young as having little to offer, and conversely the teenagers will no longer reject the wisdom of their elders simply because of age. It suggests that people will begin to listen carefully to one another without interruption or jumping to conclusions, with the belief that everyone has something to offer which can be helpful. It suggests the shifting of those prejudices behind which we have hidden for so long. Who knows? Perhaps Black soul would be good for staid, white Christian worship. It suggests that we take Paul's words seriously, that in Christ there is no slave or free, no male or female—that is, no economic or sexual barriers within the world. It suggests, also, a reorientation of one of Christianity's greatest misconceptions, that this is a Christian world. It is important that we recognize that the Christian faith is held by a minority in a world in which the non-Christian religions have gained ascendency. In that regard, the comment from Sydney Harris becomes appropriate: "The most significant aspect of the twentieth century," he writes, "overtowering all other changes, is that for the first time it is no longer a white Christian man's world." With these words the last vestige of any presumptuousness or arrogance crumbles. No longer can we, in superiority and haughtiness, remain isolated and insulated within our airtight enclaves of truth. What is more, it is obvious that God is dragging us, screaming and kicking, into a new kind of world, a world into which we may not go willingly, but a world into which we must go, if we would learn to be loving. Are we open to that?

A second important question to ask is: Do I use people for self-gain?

Let us look at this in light of the gospel, especially the life and teachings of Christ. How did the Christ deal with people? What kind of value did he put upon others? In one of the most lyrical passages within the Bible we read these words: "Have this mind among yourselves, which is yours in Christ Jesus, who . . . emptied himself, taking the form of a servant . . ." (Philippians 2:5-7). In these words we catch the theme which underlies the entire thrust of Christ's life. To all persons he was a servant who willingly gave his life a ransom for many. This does not suggest that he was a doormat, weak and naive as to the grim realities of life. Rather, he was the strong Son of God who recognized his mission from God as that of meeting the needs of people rather than manipulating them.

Now, if we could begin to see ourselves as the servants of God who are called into the world to meet the needs of persons that they might discover the fullness of life which is centered in God, life for us, and others, could distinctly change for the better. To put it another way, if we could learn to love with humility and compassion, the fullness of life of which Christ spoke could be experienced.

I'm told that when the Hellgate Bridge was built over the East River in New York, the engineers came upon an old derelict ship lying embedded in the river mud just where one of the central pieces of the bridge was to go down to its bedrock foundation. No tugboat could be found that was able to lift the wreck from its ancient resting place. It would not move, no matter what force was applied. Finally, with sudden inspiration, one of the workers took a large flatboat, which had been used to bring large stones down the river, and chained it at low tide to the old sunken ship. Then he waited for the tides to do their work. Slowly, the rising tide, with all the forces of the ocean behind it and the moon above it, came up under the flatboat, raising it inch by inch. As it came up, the wrecked ship came up with it, until it floated free of the mud that had held it. Then the barge, with its submerged load, was towed out to sea where the old water-logged ship was unchained and allowed to drop forever out of sight and reach. The power of love is a greater force than that of the tidal waves. Like the waves it has always been there. It is there now, and it has the power to lift the souls of all persons out of the ooze and mud of daily living into a new and satisfying life. But it does not work, it does not operate, until we lay hold of it to bring it into our lives. When we do, our lives take on a servant role, the work of God is done, and the needs of persons are met.

Someone has said, "It is much easier to give a person a piece of your mind than it is to give the whole of your heart." That, in so many ways, is the key sentence for our lives. If only we could offer love, compassion, and tenderness to others, the world could be visibly changed. If we trust him, God will help us to be open and active to bring that about.

Chapter 6

A FEW
MANNERS,
PLEASE!

1 Corinthians 13:5 "**Love is not . . . rude**"

A few manners, please! Surely that request strikes a responsive note within all of our hearts! One day last week, when I traveled to the Loop on the Rock Island Railroad, the need for a few manners became apparent. The train was packed. Every seat was taken. In fact, many passengers were forced to stand in the aisles all the way downtown. Some of the women had great difficulty maintaining their balance as the train swayed and lurched. But would you believe that not one of the men had the courtesy to rise and offer his seat? I felt myself saying, "A few manners, please!"

There was a similar experience in a restaurant. One evening, while at dinner, I was amazed to see a fellow diner vigorously scratch his back with his fork. I was so shocked by this breach of etiquette that I dropped a forkful of potatoes!

On the elevated train recently, a member of the younger set climbed aboard. As he made himself comfortable, he turned on his tape deck. The music, if it can be described as that, filled the train. The screams and the pounding beat pulsated against my already aching head. *What right did he have to foist his music on me?* I complained inwardly. "A few manners, please!"

Manners seem in short supply today. Once upon a time a man gave up his seat on a bus to a woman. She fainted. On recovering, she thanked the man, and he fainted. The simple rules of politeness and courtesy are not as apparent as they once were. There is little evidence that the rights and needs of others are of importance to us.

Of course, life is not as simple as it once was. How is a gentleman to act in this day of liberation? To rise in respect, to help with a coat, or to open a door may be chivalrous, but it may also prompt the tongue-lashing, "You male chauvinist pig!" It is not surprising that in this day of equality and change the safest course of action is that of hiding one's head within the newspaper and appearing preoccupied so that opportunities for common courtesies remain unnoticed.

It is here, however, that we need to look at manners from a larger perspective. Paul says, "Love is not . . . rude." At first thought, it might seem that Paul has become too meddlesome, too finicky, and too concerned with irrelevant details. What possible connection can there be between love and manners? Well, as we have learned from experience, everything in Scripture has a reason. Love and politeness are connected. For how is love to be expressed if not in behavior which is considerate and respectful? Thus, good manners become a most needed means of expressing Christian love. For it is in good manners that we show we take people seriously.

Last week I saw something loving and helpful. As I joined the throngs of commuters rushing to the Rock Island Station, I found myself intent on only one purpose. Above all, I wanted to catch the 4:55 P.M. train home. On two occasions I saw an elderly gentleman step out of the crowd, take hold of the swinging door which led into the station, and fasten it to the wall. On one occasion someone remarked to him, "Is that your good deed for the day?" Indeed it was. Like all the other commuters, he, too, was rushing for a train. He, too, could have claimed all the excuses that commuters are wont to offer. Instead, he took the time to perform a simple act of helpfulness and love. I find in this story a principle which was often revealed in our Lord's life. Time and time again, he went out of his way and endured interruptions in his schedule for the sake of others. In the Gospel of John, we read of the time when two of the Baptizer's disciples followed Jesus. The Scriptures report that "Jesus turned. . . ." That is a simple but a profound thought. Jesus took people seriously. He turned to meet them halfway; he demonstrated his concern in his behavior.

All of us are familiar with the story of the good Samaritan, of how he stopped to render aid when no one else would. The men who passed by were not bad men. In fact, they were good men whose only fault was that their values were twisted. They were on their way to church, and nothing, not even stark human need, could move them to change their schedule. Recently I read a study conducted on the campus of the Princeton Theological Seminary. Students planning to be ministers arrived at a class on preaching, only to be told that they were to go across campus to tape their sermons. Some were told that they were late and should hurry. Others were told that they could take their time. As they traveled across campus, they met a person in obvious pain and discomfort. But 60 percent of these ministerial students failed to stop and render aid. A psychiatrist commenting on the study said, "People in a hurry are less likely to help people in need." The crucial issue which emerges from this story concerns the value and importance of people. How important are people to us? Are they important enough to us that we will slow down to take them seriously, be considerate of their wishes, and act in courteous ways? Or will we rush and push our way through life, shoving others aside? The issue can be put another way: Will we love people and use things, or love things and use people? Paul leaves little doubt in his mind which is the Christian stance. Love is not rude. It takes people seriously, even to the interrupting of our lives.

Another way to love is in listening to the concerns of others. Recently I was part of an amazing conversation. A total stranger, whom I had met only minutes before, began sharing the hurts and pains of his life. He had been up until 3 o'clock that morning with his wife. She had read of some children in Chicago who had died from the Reyes Syndrome. Their daughter had just caught a cold, and the mother was frantic with fear. As the husband had held her and tried to reassure her, he had sensed that something deeper had prompted this emotional outburst. With sensitivity and tact, he had asked, "Do you feel this way because when you and your sister were young, she died from a childhood disease and you feel guilty because you lived?" As he told me this, I found myself almost incredulous. I felt that I was being invited to share in the deepest secrets of this couple. It was one of those rare, peak experiences in life where souls are bared and needs are expressed.

But suppose I had said, after the man had finished, "That's interesting, but what do you think of the Bears' chances this year?" Wouldn't that have been tragic? Unfortunately, we do it all the time. We interrupt conversations, we give advice and jump to conclusions without hearing the deepest needs of the person before us. In her book, *To Live in Love,* Eileen Guder tells of a friend who never listened. This woman "always got around to giving . . . all kinds of good advice, larded generously with Bible verses." Mrs. Guder says, "I'm sure if I told her I was having trouble keeping my grocery bill down I got some spiritual advice on that, with an appropriate quotation from the Bible. She never seemed to have problems herself, and invariably ended the conversation with something like this:

'Now, my dear, just pray about this and I'm sure the Lord will show you the way. I'm . . . glad we've had this little talk, because I always say that no matter how tired I am, I'm never too tired to help someone.'" Mrs. Guder concludes by saying, "I felt like a peon being given largesse by the bountiful lady, and I didn't like feeling that way so the friendship cooled." We can well understand that feeling, can't we? The need for our concern to be heard is great. Whenever those concerns are overlooked or at least not taken seriously, we retreat into isolation and solitude.

Needed at all times is the prayer upon our lips: "Lord, help me to listen carefully and well, not only to the words, but also to the feelings beneath the words, that I might understand and show that I care." It is in active listening that good manners are shown, love is revealed, and burdens are lifted.

A third way for us to show love in good manners is by acting appropriately. A television special presented the dramatic story of Ethel and Julius Rosenberg's trial for treason. It was a moving story which showed the ambiguities of the case, a sensitive love between a man and a woman, death by execution, and finally a penetrating comment on the death penalty. Then, instantly, a commercial was flashed upon the screen. A man was standing in his undershirt, a black spot under each arm, touting the values of a deodorant. There was nothing wrong with the commercial as such. Its offensiveness lay in its poor timing. It was tasteless, crude, and cheap. It destroyed the drama of the message which the program had labored to produce.

Unfortunately, appropriate behavior is often lacking in our lives, even within the church. One day some Christians were discussing the ways they shared their faith in Christ. One man said, "When I'm out with business associates and I'm offered a drink, I always say, 'No, thank you, I don't drink, I'm a Christian!'" No matter your views on alcohol, that manner of declining the offer is just plain rudeness and inappropriate behavior. It is that kind of pious prattle that does the Christian faith more harm than good.

We could spend a good deal of time listing the ways inappropriate behavior reveals itself within our lives. Let us take just one example. How do we act when we have been slighted or rebuffed? We will probably fit somewhere between two extremes. Either we will fight dirty, dredging up from the past all the slurs and sludge that we can recall, desperately seeking revenge and retaliation, or in suffering martyrdom we will retreat into an icy silence refusing to communicate or resolve the differences. Instead of seeking ways to resolve our problems, we compound them.

What then is appropriate behavior for us? Appropriate behavior is that which is always reaching beneath the obvious to meet a person at the point of need. Ask yourself this question: "What kind of person would I be if God gave me all I asked for?" Would you be healthy? Probably. Wealthy? Most likely. Nice? Loving? Forgiving and forgiven? Yet the whole action of God within history is not that of giving people what they desire but what they need. When God looks into the core of the human heart, he sees, not just the obvious, but the deep wants which lie unsatisfied and unmet. He sees the ugly presence of evil, the destructive power of sin, the guilty conscience, and the spirit of condemnation. He meets those needs in Jesus Christ, the Lamb which takes away the sin of the world. Now that is appropriate behavior. It is the right thing done at the right time in the right way.

In much the same way, you and I cannot be content to live on the surface of life skimming along the top in a hydrofoil existence, unaware and unconcerned for people. At all times we must seek to discover the needs and hurts of every heart that we might, even if it be in some small way, meet those needs with appropriate behavior. That is love at its best.

A cartoon in one of our daily papers showed a car traveling down a rain puddled street. On the back bumper were the words: "Have a Nice Day." But as the car passed a pedestrian, it splashed a stream of water onto the pedestrian's face. The cartoon was titled "Laughing Matter," but it was a misnomer. It is no laughing matter to live in a world where rudeness reigns. It tries one's patience and pains the soul. The world would be a much better place if only there were a few manners. For it is through manners, that love becomes real.

Chapter 7

HARD HEADS
AND
COLD HEARTS

1 Corinthians 13:5 **"Love does not insist on its own way."**

The story is told of a man who had just been promoted to a vice-president within his company. He boasted about it so continually to his wife that she finally exploded: "Vice-presidents are a dime a dozen. Why, in the supermarket they even have a vice-president in charge of prunes." Furious, the husband phoned the supermarket in the expectation of refuting his wife. He asked to speak to the vice-president in charge of prunes. The operator asked, "What kind, sir? Packaged or bulk?" While it may be farfetched to think of a vice-president in charge of prunes, it is not farfetched to remind ourselves of the specialization which has touched every part of contemporary life. In every segment of contemporary life there are those experts and consultants who claim special knowledge. While this tendency to specialize is one of our strengths, it is also one of our weaknesses. When we focus our time and energies in one direction, we cut off other parts of life and develop what may be called "tunnel vision." Tunnel vision, the *Wall Street Journal* once said, "prevents executives from seeing beyond special problems of their own department. It results in a narrow, one-sided, and inflexible view."

Tunnel vision is not only a problem faced by the executive, but it also can be found within the whole human family. One man described tunnel vision this way: "When the other fellow acts that way, he's stupid . . . when you do it, it's nerves. When he's set in his ways, he's stubborn . . . when you are, it's just firmness. When he doesn't like your friends, he's prejudiced . . . when you don't like his, you are showing good judgment of human nature. When he tries to be helpful, he's polishing the apple . . . when you do it, you are being tactful. When he takes time to do things, he's slow . . . when you take ages, you are being deliberate. When he points out difficulties, he's faultfinding . . . when you do it, you're discriminating." Tunnel vision infects every part of life in a stubborn, self-centered, and dogmatic way.

It would be naive for us to believe that tunnel vision lies outside the religious realm. Unfortunately, some of the most spectacular examples of tunnel vision have occurred within the religious life. All of us know the story of Jonah and the whale. Not so well known, however, is the remaining part of that story. Jonah is commanded by God to warn Nineveh that God will punish them if they do not mend their wicked ways. Jonah, fearful that the inhabitants of that city will repent and receive the forgiveness of God, runs away. Given a second chance by God, he preaches to the city, and the very thing he fears happens: the people repent of their sins, mend their ways, and receive the forgiveness of God. But is Jonah pleased at this outcome? Not at all! Within the hard head and cold heart of this Jewish prophet there is no room for a Gentile conversion. Jonah is a law and order man with no sense of fairness, love, or justice.

It is against such a background that the apostle Paul's words seem like the breaking of the dawn. "Love," he says, "does not insist on its own way." It isn't stubborn, self-centered, or limited in its vision. It is instead the quality of life which reaches out beyond itself in self-giving, self-forgetting love. What is needed then is the enlargement of our tunnel vision that we might learn to love. How can this happen?

We need to focus upon God. It is fascinating that the phrase "Love does not insist on its own way" should come from the apostle Paul, for Paul's life history denied those words. Listen to the speech that Paul made before King Agrippa (Acts 26:9-11).

> "I myself was convinced that I ought to do many things in opposing the name of Jesus of Nazareth. And I did so in Jerusalem; I not only shut up many of the saints in prison, by authority from the chief priests, but when they were put to death I cast my vote against them. And I punished them often in all the synagogues and tried to make them blaspheme; and in raging fury against them, I persecuted them even to foreign cities."

By Paul's own admission he was a tyrant, possessed with demonic tunnel vision. He could see nothing but revenge clothed with a mask of piety. But yet, he came to the place where he was able to say, "Love does not insist on its own way"! What brought Paul to that point? Did he finally see the destructiveness of his tunnel vision? Did he finally understand the tragedy of a life which is too narrowly defined? The answer is recorded for us in one of the most dramatic conversion stories within the New Testament. As Paul journeyed to Damascus in pursuit of the Christians, a blinding flash of light exploded from heaven and a compelling voice addressed his soul, and Paul, the heroic avenger of the true faith lay sightless and humiliated upon the ground. What was the light? What was the voice? It was Christ! God met Paul face to face on the road to Damascus, and in that meeting the radical transformation of his soul took place. Nevermore could Paul be content with a narrow and limited view on life. By the grace and mercy of God, Paul's life was enlarged and increased.

Some years ago the actress Mary Pickford wrote a book called *Why Not Try God?* There was a sense in which the title was offensive, for it implied that God was little different from other resources to be consumed. But a great truth was contained in that title in that it pointed seeking hearts in the right direction. Do we wish to know how to love? Try God! Do we desire that experience of power which can transform our lives? Try God! God, the One whom Jesus called Father, possesses the capacity to expand our tunnel vision, soften our hard heads, and melt our cold, cold hearts.

The question must be asked, however: How can this happen? How can God rescue us from our stubborn and uncompromising ways of living? The answer is suggested in the story of a spider who built his web high up among the rafters of a barn. He started by spinning a long, thin thread which he attached to the end of one of the beams. With this thread still attached to him, the spider jumped off the beam and spun out more thread on the way down, until he reached the place he planned as the center of his web. From the center he then spun out other threads like the spokes of a wheel, attaching each of them to the walls and other places. Finally, he had an exquisitely made web that helped him catch many fine fat flies. But, unfortunately, the spider grew fat, lazy, and vain. One day as he was admiring the web, he noticed the long, fine thread that he had first spun from the top beam. He said, "I wonder what that is for? I can't imagine why I even put it there. It doesn't catch any flies." On a sudden impulse he broke the thread. As a result the wonderful web collapsed. The spider had forgotten that the one thread, the link to the beam above, had supported the whole web. The same truth is real within the lives of people. Our only hope of being saved from the lovelessness which limits and destroys our lives is found in keeping the divine connection with God that allows his generous and extravagant love to flow into our lives. It is then we are given the power to rise above our stubborn and dogmatic ways.

Secondly, we can learn to deal with such stubbornness by finding a great spiritual purpose in life. One of the reasons which prompted the coming of Jesus into the world was the lifting of individuals' vision to include other people. A man who had come to the big city from his small hometown had climbed the ladder of success and wealth. Now with the means and freedom to indulge himself, he thought of his hometown and how nice it would be to return for a visit, a visit no doubt characterized by praise and adulation of the local boy who had made the big time. When he stepped off the train, there was no welcoming committee to greet him. This was surprising and a bit disconcerting. The few people on the platform ignored him and went on their way. As he picked up his bags, one of the old men of the town came by. He looked at him curiously and asked, "Howdy, Jim, you leavin' town?" There is a strong tendency for all of us to live as if we were the center of the universe. We seek, as the result of our lovelessness, to be, among the millions of the world, number one. It is here that the empire builder tries to overcome his littleness by the grasping of power. It is here that the Don Juan seeks to satisfy his emptiness through sexual conquests. Love and poeple are not preeminent. Power and control are the only realities which count.

When Jesus recommended: "Seek . . . first the kingdom of God, and his righteousness; and all these things shall be added unto you" (Matthew 6:33), he was expressing a precious truth. He knew that life could only take on meaning whenever persons moved out beyond the limits of their own skins to find a center in something other than themselves. Thus, he said in effect, "Find a great spiritual purpose in life to which you can give yourself unreservedly and wholeheartedly. Then, the things you want, the things you really want, shall become yours."

It has been said that there are only two kinds of people in this world: those who think of their rights, privileges, and what life owes them; and those who think of their duties, responsibilities, and what they owe life. All the difference in the world can be found between these two contradictory styles of life. To concentrate upon oneself is to die the death of selfishness and pride. To focus upon life's challenges and others is the beginning of joy.

During the last war, a young bride from the East followed her husband to an army camp on the edge of the desert in California. Living conditions were primitive at best and he had advised against her coming, but she wanted to be with him. The only housing they could find was a run-down shack near an Indian village. The heat was unbearable in the daytime, 115° in the shade. The wind blew constantly spreading dust and sand all over everything. The days were long and boring. Her only neighbors were the Indians, none of whom spoke English. When her husband was ordered farther into the desert for two weeks of maneuvers, loneliness and the wretched living conditions got the best of her. She wrote to her mother that she was coming home; she just couldn't take any more. In a short time she received a reply which included these two lines:

Two men looked out from prison bars.
One saw mud, the other saw stars.

She read the lines over and over and began to feel ashamed of herself. She didn't really want to leave her husband. All right, she'd look for the stars. In the following days she set out to make friends with the Indians. She asked them to teach her weaving and pottery. At first they were distant; but as soon as they sensed her interest was genuine, they returned her friendship. She became fascinated with their culture and history, in fact, everything about them.

She began to study the desert as well, and soon it, too, changed from a desolate, forbidding place to a marvelous thing of beauty. She had her mother send her books. She studied the forms of the cacti, the yuccas, and the Joshua trees. She collected seashells that had been left there millions of years ago when the sands had been an ocean floor. Later, she became such an expert on the area that she wrote a book about it.

What had changed? Not the desert and certainly not the Indians. They were as they had been for thousands of years. It was the way the woman began to look upon life that had changed. She had expanded her life to reach beyond herself and in the process found something worth living for. That's what Jesus was getting at with his exhortation to seek first the kingdom of God. If we can learn those high and holy principles of Christ, which move us beyond ourselves, there can be hope and love.

There is a famous conversation recorded between two Christian persons. As they argued one day, arriving at no solution, one of the Christians remarked in desperation: "All right, then. You do it your way! I'll do it His!" The arrogant, insistent spirit is little short of destructive. When we connect ourselves to God and live for the great spiritual purposes in life, there is hope that our hard heads and cold hearts will be transformed and love will become a reality.

Chapter 8

QUIT
BUGGING
ME

1 Corinthians 13:5 "**Love . . . is not irritable.**"

"Love . . . is not irritable." With these words the apostle Paul
focused upon the humanness of our lives. One day two women were
talking. One asked, "Did you get up grouchy this morning?" "No,"
replied the other, "I let him sleep!" Irritableness, grouchiness, and
touchiness find a lodging place within all our hearts. They do not
need to be learned. They are everyday responses to life.

How is that irritable spirit revealed within our lives? One of the
most common irritations in family life is centered around the
toothpaste tube. Family discord is certain if one member is a pusher,
another a squeezer, and another a roller. Do you leave the cap on or
off? Do you work from the bottom of the tube or the middle? Strange,
isn't it, that such a simple thing could be the cause of so much trouble?

One of my pet peeves is related to the express lane in the
supermarket. The sign above the lane says, "Eight items or less only."
Do you know what I do? I stand there counting the number of items
in the baskets around me. When I spot someone with nine or ten or
eleven or more items, I find myself becoming irritated. I have even
been known to say out loud, "Express lane—eight items or less!" The
editor of a modern almanac conducted a peeve poll to see what
irritated his readers. A large number of people expressed their dislike
with rude, stupid drivers; dull, lazy salesclerks; bad grammar; people
who pronounce the "s" in Illinois; and return envelopes too small for
the material to be returned in them. Well, the list of life's irritations

45

could continue endlessly. No part of life is immune. Everything is subject to the petty, grouchy, and irritable spirit.

All this may sound terribly trivial when the weighty subject of love is under discussion. But it isn't. The petty annoyances and minor frustrations in life have the power to destroy love. When we lose our tempers, we lose everything.

Paul says that "love . . . is not irritable." The King James Version translates this phrase to say, "[Love] . . . is not easily provoked." That, however, is an incorrect translation. The word "easily" does not appear within the best manuscripts. It is a later addition from some scribe who wished an easier understanding of love. Love is not provoked, period. There is no room for irritation and touchiness within love at all.

The problem is crucial. How can we deal with that grumpy, grouchy, irritable spirit which plays such a large role within our lives? The answer begins with awareness of ourselves.

Why do we become grouchy? Dr. Harold Visotsky, chairman of the Department of Psychiatry at Northwestern University, calls grouchiness "a very common complaint." He goes on to say that the reasons for grouchiness are as varied as personalities are. "Being grouchy is like having a headache," he says; "it could be due to a brain tumor, hangover, fatigue, argument, anything." Someone has suggested that there are three spiritual reasons for an irritable spirit. When wounded vanity, real or imagined injustice, or blocked behavior are experienced, grouchiness is not far behind. There once was a secretary who became concerned about the change in her personality from easygoing to grouchy. It turned out that she and her best friend had been promoted from the secretarial pool to private secretaries. That friendship continued until the friend was promoted to executive secretary. The woman then became alienated from her friend due to the spirit of wounded pride which became lodged within her heart.

The first step in dealing with the grouchiness which besets us is to search our souls and to become aware of those factors within us which make us grouchy. When the apostle Paul recorded the Lord's Supper within the Scriptures, he said, "Let a man examine himself. . . ." Paul knew, as we are now beginning to discover, that the unexamined life is not worth living. Close attention must be given to our behavior. Motives must be examined. Every part of our life's experience must come under scrutiny to see what triggers the irritable behavior within us. That procedure may not always be pleasurable, for we may see some things we do not like. We may find ourselves in the situation of the wicked stepmother in *Snow White and the Seven*

Dwarfs. You will recall that she said to the mirror, "Mirror, mirror on the wall, who is the fairest of them all?" And the mirror replied, "Snow White." Sometimes the truth is hard to take, but it is founded upon a simple and fundamental fact: it is better to understand one's feelings than it is to ventilate. Most persons have a tendency to express rather than examine their grouchiness. That endeavor, however, has no saving power. As James (1:20) puts it: "for the anger of man does not work the righteousness of God." In fact the ventilation of our irritable spirits, the dumping of internal garbage, only contradicts what our hearts desire: a solution to the problems we face and the creation of relationships of love with God and others. Examination for the purpose of awareness is the starting point for love.

The second principle in dealing with our irritability lies in self-control. There is an important word for us from the Book of Proverbs:

> "He who is slow to anger is better than the mighty,
> and he who rules his spirit than he who takes a city."
> Proverbs 16:32

In other words, it is not enough to examine and understand the causes of our critical spirit. Self-control and discipline are needed to move our lives in a positive direction. Wheeling the baby buggy along, a young father seemed to be trying to comfort his howling infant: "That's a good boy, Clarence. Easy does it, Clarence. Control yourself, Clarence." A young mother noticed the situation and remarked, "You must be wonderful father. You seem to understand little Clarence." The father interrupted, "The baby's name is Horace; I'm Clarence."

The need, which lies within the hearts of all persons, is that of bringing under control these vagrant spirits which have the capacity to destroy and disrupt joyous living. As long as the irritable feelings and grouchy, grumpy spirits are permitted to reign supreme without the checks and balances of control, there is little hope that our lives will ever reveal the quality of love. The end result will be a total capitulation to the spirit of irritability and the destruction of all that is loving and godly. Let me share with you an experience which comes from a small group of which I am a part. We have learned that our capacity for self-deception is enormous. We are able to rationalize any action and evade any issue by offering feeble excuses and wallowing in self-pity. Therefore, we have agreed to be accountable to one other person in the group. Every two weeks we tell that other person the particular problem on which we feel concerned to work. Then, two weeks later, we share with that same person how we have fared. If we evade the problem, if we engage in evasive tactics, we shall be challenged. We have deliberately placed ourselves in a situation where we can be subject to the examination and scrutiny of other persons. Now, it is that kind of accountability which is needed to offset the grumpy, grouchy spirit. Only as our lives are brought under control and dampers are placed on our irritable moods can we grow to the place where love becomes preeminent within us.

The third way to deal with our irritable spirit is by making allowances for people. One of the enormous rationalizations surrounding our lives lies in the way we tend to believe that most everything we do to others is accidental, while what is done to us by others is deliberate. One of my favorite stories concerns a fellow pastor. One week he was on a speaking engagement in a distant city. When morning came, he left his hotel room and went to the restaurant for breakfast. The waitress bustled up to him, offered him no word of greeting, and gruffly took his order. As she left, the minister thought to himself: "That's the grumpiest woman I've seen in a long time." The next morning was the same, but now the pastor was getting concerned, for he felt she shouldn't affect him this way. During the next few days he made a deliberate attempt to get beneath her gruff exterior. He found she was more than willing to talk. She was divorced, trying to raise her four children by herself, and caring for her invalid mother. On the last day, the minister said to her: "You know, when I first met you, I said to myself, 'There is the grumpiest-looking person I've seen in a long time.'" "That's funny," the waitress replied, "When I saw you that first morning, that's what I said about you!"

Why do people act the way they do? Are they deliberately seeking to malign our spirits, destroy our faith, and get under our skin? Well, of course, there will always be a small minority of persons who engage in vicious attacks and destructive behavior. But for the most part, people are so wrapped up in their own lives, their problems, and difficulties, that they are unaware of the impact their lives have on others.

For that reason love demands that we should learn to make allowances for people. In a church there was a poignant statement affixed to the pulpit: "Be tender, in every pew there is at least one broken heart." If that is true within the church, it is equally true within the family, the classroom, the office, and the car in front of you. When we learn to see people as flesh and blood humans who are struggling through perplexing difficulties and agonizing problems, love will become a possibility for our lives.

We cannot possibly deal with our irritability without depending

6. DO A LOVING THING

Love Is—Not Rude

This week I will remind myself seven times that I need
to act courteously to those persons I meet.

1   2   3   4   5   6   7

_____

(signed)

---

7. DO A LOVING THING

Love—Does Not Insist On Its Own Way

____This week I will try to resist the urge to dominate
others.

____I will try to understand the point of view of people
who differ from me.

____I will thank God daily for his patience with my
stubbornness.

_____

(signed)

---

8. DO A LOVING THING

Love Is—Not Irritable

____This week I will spend time trying to understand
why I allow things to "bug" me.

____With God's help I will seek to understand the
point of view of those who irritate me.

____I will pray daily for those who irritate me.

_____

(signed)

9. DO A LOVING THING

Love Is—Not Resentful

____I will make a deliberate effort this week to "forgive and forget."

____I will take a step of reconciliation toward a person with whom I have a problem.

____I will remind myself of the cross—of God's love and mercy toward me.

_____
(signed)

---

10. DO A LOVING THING

Love—Rejoices in the Right

____I will work hard this week to see others as they are and myself as I am.

____I will try to affirm rather than condemn others this week.

____I will seek to let God love others through me this week.

_____
(signed)

upon the divine resource of prayer. One day a minister was dressing to begin an afternoon of pastoral calling. When he could not find his cuff links, he began to storm around the house. Eventually he found them, finished dressing, and left his wife in tears. First, he called upon an old man who had been stricken for years with arthritis. He was patient and cheerful, even though the pain was intense. Then he called upon a young boy whose body was filled with cancer. Yet from his lips there radiated a love for Christ and a commitment to him. Next, he visited a family on relief. As he entered their rundown shack, he could hear the family repeat the familiar words: "Our Father, who art in heaven. . . ." Then he visited a young couple whose only child had recently died. They were in deep sorrow but not despair. They spoke of the resurrection and of life eternal through Jesus Christ. When the minister went home, he was deeply impressed with the power of Christ to deal with all of life's problems. He said to his wife, "What a wonderful thing is the grace of God! There is nothing too hard for it." "Yes," replied his wife, "It is wonderful indeed, but there is one thing that it does not seem to have the power to accomplish." The minister was startled. "What can that be?" he asked. His wife answered, "It does not seem to have the power to control the minister's temper when his cuff links are misplaced."

Can the power of God's grace change our irritable spirits into love? Yes, when we pray. Prayer is that marvelous resource which brings the power of God's grace into the depths of our lives and into every relationship. How can we continue an irritable spirit when we pray? Think of the person who bothers you the most. Pray for that person. Ask God to help you love him or her and see what happens. If your desire is truthful, and your prayer is honest, it will be impossible for you to continue your grouchy, irritable spirit. Instead, you will find yourself expressing the words of Jesus from the cross: "Father, forgive them, for they know not what they do." Your life will be changed. Your relationships with others will become deeper, and your relationship with God will be strengthened. Prayer is a mighty resource which has the power to overcome life's annoyances and petty irritations.

It was said of John Wesley, the founder of the Methodist Church, that the secret of his power was "his kingly neglect of trifles." He could ignore the small irritations which would keep most people awake half the night. With quiet poise he could endure uncomfortable inns, the frustrations of a lame horse, and the cantankerousness of liverymen. He felt that all these things had no business getting in the way of his main business. These were things to be mastered, not things to master life.

There, it would seem, is the challenge which lies before us. Will we allow the irritations of life to master us? Or, will we master them? At stake are our lives. At stake is love.

Chapter 9

THE CHIP
ON
MY
SHOULDER

1 Corinthians 13:5 "**Love . . . is not . . . resentful.**"

Recently, I heard a story which concerned a family living on an Illinois farm. Life was simple then, and faith was a clear-cut, straightforward thing as it was taught and preached in the little country church. One received Christ as one's Savior and then one lived with Christ as the Lord of life. That commitment and pilgrimage was the dynamic of that family, especially the mother.

The neighbors next to this family were a sorry lot. They were gossipy and malicious, noisy and quarrelsome. The children were addicted to the appropriation of the property of others, which is a gentle way of saying that they were a pack of junior-sized thieves. Collectively, they were a thorn in the flesh of the neighborhood.

Growing between the two houses, on the first family's land and shading the neighbor's kitchen window, was the most miserable skeleton of a peach tree that had ever grown. Every spring the gnarled old tree would, with great effort, gather together all its little store of strength and produce a few leaves and a few blossoms. In due season the blossoms would develop into tiny, hard, green peaches that never matured. They were good for only one thing—throwing. You can guess who threw them, and where. The tree was so completely unproductive that the mother decided to have it cut down and to put flowers in its place.

It wasn't long before the word of her decision reached the neighbors. They rushed over to plead with her to permit the old tree to stand because it was the only shade they had over their kitchen. Their kitchen had a flat roof, and it was exposed to the merciless Illinois sun. It was a tempting picture, those rascals sweltering in their doubly heated kitchen. There was certainly poetic justice in it; they had turned the heat on others often enough and one could easily be tempted to see a prophetic element in the situation. But this mother was a Christian who believed she ought to act like one. She said, "Of course, I'll leave the tree." And she did.

When spring came, something wonderful happened to the tree. Those bony, old limbs disappeared under a great cloud of blossoms. The blossoms developed into the tiny, hard, green peaches that the family had known across the years, and then, wonder of wonders, they matured to become sweet, delicious fruit. The family ate all they could; some were given to the neighbors, including the unpleasant ones, and the remainder were canned for the winter.

That tree had never produced good fruit before; it never produced good fruit again, for it died the next year. Its glory may have been due to the weather or to some chemical, but to the family there was an unmistakable reason: the mother had had an opportunity to return evil for evil and get even. Instead, she had sown love, and from that love there came forth a most wonderful harvest.

This story speaks directly to our hearts. Paul may declare that "love is not resentful," but that hardly dispels the bitter feelings within us which yearn for retaliation and revenge. There is a tendency for many of us to live as spiritual accountants, keeping careful records of the slights and offenses which we experience.

It is little wonder that all our relationships are tinged with disorder. The tendency to brood over our wrongs and to nurse our wounds blocks the love of God from acting within our lives and prevents the love relationships which we desperately seek. How can we deal with this vital issue of resentment? Can we find a way to love?

We can begin by practicing the art of selective forgetfulness. One evening a man was passing through a hotel lobby when he spied an old school chum. The two hadn't seen each other for years and their meeting was the occasion of laughter and joy. They spent the evening together remembering the good old days and all the old escapades. It was late when the man returned home, and he knew his wife would be more than angry that he had been gone so long. The next morning he met his old friend for breakfast. The friend asked, "How did it go with your wife?" "Oh, she got historical," the man replied. "You mean hysterical, don't you?" said the friend. "No, historical," the man replied. "When I got home, she told me everything I had ever done wrong."

What do we keep in our memories? Oscar Wilde once described memory "as the diary that we all carry about with us." How tragic it is that for so many of us the diary is filled with daily entries of hurts and attacks, slights and grievances. No matter whether the words are said in jest or in ignorance, the resentful spirit filters the words in only one way—as a personal attack and denunciation. They are written forever within the diary of our souls. Someone graphically described such a tendency as he saw it within Pope Paul IV: "He never forgot such incidents, which was one of his fundamental weaknesses. He might bury the hatchet for a time, but he gave the impression of always carefully marking the spot."

Harry Emerson Fosdick once said, "Blessed is the life that does not collect resentments. . . ." But we might well ask, how is it possible to overcome the tendency for revenge and retaliation? One way is that of developing the art of selective forgetfulness. By all the strength we can muster and by all the grace God can provide, we need to train our memories to recall those things which have the capacity to make us more godly and Christlike and to repel those destructive traits which ruin love.

What I am emphasizing is a glorious biblical truth. You and I, by the authority of God's creation, are to take charge of our own lives. No longer dare we permit the malignancy of resentment to run rampant through our souls. With decisiveness we must destroy its presence. We must determine within ourselves that we will no longer remain trapped within the destructive despair of our critical and faultfinding spirit, interpreting every word and deed as a deliberate slight and attack. We must force ourselves, by a conscious act of the will, to change our entire outlook and manner.

It was this, I believe, that the apostle Paul had in mind when he wrote to the church at Rome and said: "Do not be conformed to this world but be transformed by the renewal of your mind . . ." (12:2). It was also, I believe, what Paul meant when in writing to the church at Philippi he said, "Finally, brethren, whatever is true . . . honorable . . . just . . . pure . . . lovely . . . gracious . . . if there is any excellence . . . anything worthy of praise . . . *think* about these things" (4:8). What focus will our minds have? Will they recall the past with all its injuries, supposed and real? Or will the focus look for the best that is to be found? This is no Pollyanna solution. It is no avoidance of the pain and hurt which life often brings. Rather, it is the realization that by the retraining and transformation of our minds the resentful spirit can be destroyed.

At her golden wedding celebration, the wife told the guests the secret of her happy marriage. "On my wedding day," she said, "I decided to make a list of ten of my husband's faults which, for the sake of the marriage, I would overlook." As the guests were leaving, a young girl, whose marriage had recently been in difficulty, asked the grandmother what some of the faults were that she had seen fit to overlook. The wife said, "To tell you the truth, my dear, I never did get around to listing them. But whenever my husband did something that made me hopping mad, I would say to myself, 'Lucky for him that's one of the ten!'"

You and I, if we so desire, can choose to live with the same directness of purpose and seriousness of intention. It isn't easy, but it can be done. When it is, resentment is curtained and love becomes supreme.

Resentment can also be eased by focusing upon the quality of forgiveness. When we deal with such a bitter spirit as resentment, it is important to remember that the Christian faith is founded, not upon justice, but mercy. Peter said to his Lord, feeling very magnanimous: "Lord, how many times should we forgive—seven?" Jesus replied, "Seventy times seven." The response of Jesus to Peter's question reveals the spendthrift character of God's grace and the extravagant quality of forgiveness. Life, from God's point of view, is not to be lived on a tit-for-tat, eye-for-eye, tooth-for-tooth basis. That is too limited for love. Life must be clothed with the cloak of mercy and garbed with the generosity of grace. Unlimited forgiveness to those who offend us, slight us, and attack us is the Christian way. As Paul wrote in the book of Colossians (3:13, J. B. Phillips): "Forgive as freely as the Lord has forgiven you."

This, however, is no recommendation for a passive doormat approach to life. It is, in fact, just the opposite. To forgive your enemies takes greater courage than to kill them; to love those who manipulate and use you is far more difficult than to attack them; to pray for those who despitefully use you, as Jesus commanded us, is a far better quality than seeking revenge and retaliation.

It is in that sense that forgiveness is a costly commodity. When we look at the cross and see the extent to which God was willing to go that we might be set free from our sins, we see something of the pain of forgiveness. When we think of issuing forgiveness to those who have offended us and hurt us, we can feel our mouths becoming dry and our breasts pounding. Anything, we cry, but not that! The forgiveness God demands is too costly, too great, too much beyond us!

Let me for a moment compound the problem. It is one of the comforting Bible truths that not only does God forgive us of our sins but that he also forgets our sins. Isaiah (43:25) puts it this way: "I, even I, am he that blotteth out thy transgressions for mine own sake, and will not remember thy sins." Can we do the same? Can we forgive and forget? As long as we remember our hurts and at each new quarrel or disagreement trot out the old complaints, we show we have not freely forgiven at all. Love means forgiveness, and forgiveness to be real must involve forgetfulness.

During World War II, eighteen-year-old Pvt. Robert Johnstone had a premonition that he might be killed in battle. He asked his parents that, if he did not return from the war, they use his government life insurance to establish a scholarship for a Japanese student in the United States at the war's end. Shortly thereafter, Pvt. Johnstone was killed on Luzon. Three years later, *Life* magazine featured a picture story of Robert Nishiyama, a Japanese Christian and former suicide pilot, depicting his life as a freshman at Lafayette College in Pennsylvania. His roommate was an ex-marine, studying for the ministry; his best friend, another freshman, was Bruce Johnstone, younger brother of his benefactor. Robert Nishiyama graduated from Lafayette with an excellent scholastic record; he was active in the college church and became an outstanding Christian leader. During these college years he spent all his holidays with the Johnstone family who had learned the healing power of Christian forgiveness.

Is that too much to ask? Is that quality of forgiveness beyond our capacity and coping power? Are we too human to forgive and forget? Well, no matter how we respond to these difficult questions, the promise of the Christian faith is that there is a superhuman power available to us in the love and the power of God. Jesus Christ, the ever-present and all-powerful One can change our inner lives and resentful spirits to make forgiving and forgetting possible. He can, if we will but let him, work his transforming miracle of love within us. Yes, it is costly. Yes, it is difficult. But it is the secret of the best-lived life.

One man said: "Forgiveness does not change the past, but it does enlarge the future." Is that not our concern, to live to the hilt in the days before us? Let us become selective in our memories and enthusiastic in the art of forgiving. With the power and help of God, the chip on our shoulders can be removed and we can learn to love.

Chapter 10

THE
HEALING
POWER
OF LOVE

1 Corinthians 13:6 **"Love . . . rejoices in the right."**

Once there was a tourist who was forced to stop in a country town for engine repairs. The elderly mechanic at the only garage "fixed" the car by tapping the engine twice with a hammer. The tourist was then presented with a bill for $100. After he had heard the customer's complaint, the mechanic said, "If it will make you any happier, I'll itemize the bill: two dollars for the two taps of the hammer and the other $98 for knowing where to tap."

As we come to the last of love's descriptions, it is obvious that the apostle Paul knows right where to tap. Our hearts have been deeply touched as we have learned how much better it is to be patient than impatient, and how important it is to be kind. We have been confronted with the tragic human tendencies of jealousy, boasting, arrogance, and rudeness—all of which destroy love. We have learned that love is not self-centered, irritable, or resentful. Indeed, Paul knows exactly where to tap in his description of love.

Moffatt clearly translates Paul's words when he says: "Love is never glad when others go wrong; love is . . . always eager to believe the best." With these words the penetrating insights of the Apostle come crushing in upon us. If there is any evil tendency which lies within us, it is the malicious enjoyment which comes when something derogatory is learned about someone else. Our ears lust for some spicy word of gossip. With relish we treat ourselves to the story of another's misfortunes. With spiteful embellishment, we pass the story on.

The difficulty in dealing with this evil spirit is the awareness that there is sufficient justice in our position to delude ourselves into thinking we are entirely justified. It is wrong for a husband and a wife to say unkind things about the other in public; it is wrong for a friend to break an engagement because someone more important asked him to do something. It is from such a genuine grievance that vindictiveness quickly arises. In retaliation we strike back crying with a voice filled with self-righteousness, "He had it coming to him."

The challenge before us, however, is to bring this unlovely, critical spirit under the healing power of love. With all the strength that we can muster and with all the power that God can give, we need to reach out to others eager, not for their worst, but for their best, that love might reign supreme.

We can begin by seeing ourselves as we are. Recently, I read the report of an explorer who visited the Negritos of the Philippine Islands. He said: "The trip entailed a long hike up a mountain, with the thermometer at 125 degrees. I could not eat and could hardly breathe. My companions spread a lunch under the trees. As they ate, an old man, ugly and blotched with sores, approached and looked on. A newspaper man in our party said: 'There's the most hideous human being I have ever seen. I have traveled in South America and all over the South Seas, but I have never seen a human being nearer an animal than that old beast.' Suddenly, the old fellow disappeared and returned with a huge palm leaf for me to fan; and noting me ill, pointed for me to lie down. He disappeared again and returned with a tube of spring water from which he filled a bamboo cup for me to drink from. After lunch was over, one of the party gave him a sandwich. He looked at it hungrily, but gave it to a mother with a child. Another was given him, but he handed it to an old woman. The third he gave to a hungry old man. He passed more around, until all of the starving people had been fed. Finally he ate. And yet, only a few moments before, we, in our wonder, had described this ugly old man as 'the nearest to animal of any human being we knew.'" It is an unfortunate human tendency which prompts us to look down our noses at others, to find faults in others, to locate reasons to judge others, and at the same time to ignore the state of our own lives. One man said, "To speak ill of others is a dishonest way of praising ourselves, if we only knew it." And, he was right.

It was this evasive human tendency which caused Jesus to include the penetrating words in the Sermon on the Mount: "Judge not, that you be not judged. . . . Why do you see the speck that is in your brother's eye but do notice the log that is in your own eye?" (Matthew 7:1-3). Commentators have pointed to these words as an illustration of the humor of the Christ. The contrast between a speck and a log is ludicrous. But there is little humor in these words. They are all too true. The human tendency is to evade seeing ourselves as we are and to focus upon the sin, the foibles, the mistakes, and the failures of another. Sydney Harris once put it this way: "Truth is the one commodity that always seems to be in great demand and scarce supply, when the truth about truth is exactly the opposite: the supply is unlimited, but the demand is very scarce, for what we want are facts that will make us feel more comfortable, not facts that free us from our enslavement to self."

Love, however, demands the truth. Love cannot flourish in a climate of secrecy, evasion, and dishonesty. Although the experience will at times be less than pleasant and perhaps even ego-shattering, love necessitates that we see ourselves for what we are, sinners with logs in our eyes who, along with the rest of humanity, desperately need the grace and mercy of God. That is the beginning point for love to become real.

A second task which lies before us is that of setting others free. A few months after moving to a small town, a woman complained to a neighbor about the poor service at the local drugstore. She hoped the new acquaintance would repeat her complaint to the owner. The next time she went to the drugstore, the druggist greeted her with a big smile and told her how happy he was to see her again. He said he hoped she liked their town and please to let him know if there was anything he could do to help her and her husband get settled. He then filled her order promptly and efficiently. Later the woman repeated the miraculous change to her friend. "I suppose you told the druggist how poor I thought the service was?" she asked. "Well, no," the woman replied. "In fact, and I hope you don't mind, I told him you were amazed at the way he had built up this small town drugstore and that you thought it was one of the best run drugstores you'd ever seen." There is a vital truth in this story which can be illustrated time and time again from the life of our Lord. Do you remember the first meeting between Jesus and Simon Peter? (John 1:42, TEV) "Jesus looked at him and said, 'You are Simon, the son of John. Your name will be Cephas.' (This is the same as Peter, and means 'Rock.')" Now, Jesus could have given Peter a thorough and detailed analysis of all his sins and faults, but he didn't. Instead, with great wisdom, he focused upon the possibilities and the potential which he could see within him. Thus, to weak, vacillating, and cowardly Peter, Jesus gave a vision of the person he could become. He offered him hope that one day he could be as magnificent as a mountain and as reliable as a rock. In one of the other stirring accounts of our Lord's life we read of the distraught woman taken in adultery (John 8:1-11). To this woman, who in so many ways had been used to serve lesser ends, Jesus lovingly said, "Who has condemned you?" When the woman replied, "No one," Jesus responded, "Neither do I condemn you, go and sin no more." Once again, Jesus could have denounced this woman for her actions and even condemned her. Yet, Jesus, looking into her heart, saw that she was condemned enough. He offered her a second chance to make good in life and, in so doing, set her free.

The strain of truth which runs through these two stories from the Scripture is one which our hearts desperately need to hear and practice: Affirmation, not condemnation, is the spiritual gift which sets people free to fulfill their unique God-given potential. The critical, faultfinding, narrow, mistake-pointing-out spirit has no power to set free. Only an accepting love possesses such power. Once there was a man who, because of a series of difficulties, was forced to sell pencils around the subways of Manhattan. An elderly banker dropped a quarter into the beggar's outstretched hand, turned to go, hesitated, and then returned to say: "I want to apologize for treating you like a beggar. You are a businessman, of course, and I came back to get the pencils I paid for." The astonished beggar handed the banker two pencils and thanked him with wonder. Many months later the banker stopped at a small stationery store on the outer fringe of Wall Street. As he was about to leave, after making a few minor purchases, the proprietor stopped him and said, "I'm sure you won't remember me, but I will never forget you. Some time ago I was a subway beggar with a handful of pencils, and you called me a businessman. That remark gave me back my self-respect. From then on I refused gifts and really sold pencils, lots of them and good ones, too. From that sidewalk business I saved my money, borrowed a bit more, and then opened this little shop. I'm beginning to make a go of it. And all because of a few words from you." Words of affirmation and encouragement are needed within this world. When uttered with love, people are set free.

Third, we can be saved from an unloving, critical spirit by becoming open channels of God's love. If there is any single truth about love, it is that it cannot be contained. Love, to be real, must be shared with others. Often we wonder why God created the world. The answer is found in love. According to the New Testament, "God is love" (1 John 4:16), and love to be real must have an object to love. Thus, God created the world. The same principle is also true on the human level. Love is never real in the abstract. It must take on the flesh and bones of loving people. There is a story told of the conversion of D. L. Moody. When Moody entered the Mt. Vernon

Sunday School, Superintendent Palmer assigned him to a class of boys taught by Mr. Edward Kimball. Moody appeared desperately needy to his teacher. So, on the morning of April 21, 1855, Mr. Kimball went down to the shoe store where Moody worked. Moody was in the back of the store wrapping shoes. The Sunday school teacher put his hand on his shoulder and made what he described later as a "weak appeal." Years later he said, "I never could remember just what I did say; something about Christ and his love; that was all." Moody was to write, as a world-famous evangelist, "I can feel his hand yet!" It was a touch and a word of love from a stammering Sunday school teacher which made the difference in the life of that young boy. It is precisely the same kind of love which is desperately needed within the hearts of people today. Somehow, we need to learn how to reach out to those about us and, even with stammering, halting speech, become the channels through which God's love may flow.

Unfortunately, many of us feel that such a loving way lies beyond our grasp. We are like the Indian who was sending a smoke signal to his tribe in New Mexico when a terrific explosion not only interrupted him, but also sent him flying into a ditch twenty yards away. It was an atomic bomb experiment, and the Indian pulled himself together in time to see the mushroom smoke billow into the sky. He watched in awe-struck silence for a moment and then clucked his tongue as he murmured: "I wish I'd said that!" We may feel that a ministry of love is beyond our ability and power. We may wish to express the words and actions of love, but feel incapable of such a task. However, it is important, vitally important, that we begin to understand that our task in life as Christian persons is not so much to be sufficient in meeting the needs of people as it is to be the open channels through which God's love may flow through us to others. To put it another way, the Christ who lives within our hearts by faith is seeking to live his life of love through us. He will, if we will but let him, love people through us.

An unknown author has said: "We are not responsible for being the persons we are. God made us who we are; that is fixed forever. We might wish God had made us differently, but no amount of wishing can make much change. Thus, our business in life is to take ourselves in hand and see what we can make out of the selves we are. And, in spite of our limited and handicapped selves, we can make a contribution to the world." These words are particularly true in relationship to love. We can love in the way Paul describes love. When we see ourselves clearly, seek to set others free, and live as the channels of God's love to others, then love can become real.

TRY RATING YOURSELF AGAINST 1 CORINTHIANS 13

(Maximum rating of 10 points for each)

LOVE IS PATIENT

Patience is defined as self-control, even under provocation; bearing pains or trials without complaint; having forbearance for the shortcomings of others.

Enter your patience rating. _____

LOVE IS KIND

A kind person is considerate of the feelings of others and always endeavors, even if it involves effort or sacrifice, to do those things which help people or make them happier.

Enter your kindness rating. _____

LOVE IS NOT JEALOUS

A jealous person is inclined to resent the success of anyone who has accomplished more than he has, and to attribute the other person's success to luck, "pull," or even dishonesty.

How do you rate yourself on being free of such jealousy? _____

LOVE IS NOT BOASTFUL

Many people regularly do a fine, generous thing and then spoil it all by boasting of how thoughtful they are—as if demanding praise in payment for their kindness.

How do you rate yourself on being free of such boastfulness? _____

LOVE IS NOT ARROGANT
Arrogant persons are aggressively disposed to claim for themselves more consideration than is their due. They delight in "lording" it over such people as servants, employees, salespeople in stores, etc.
How free of arrogance are you? _____

LOVE IS NOT RUDE
Love is courteous. It is considerate of the rights and feelings of others.
How do you rate yourself on courtesy? _____

LOVE DOES NOT INSIST ON ITS OWN WAY
Out of sheer obstinacy and the desire to dominate, many will insist that either something be done *their* way, or they will have no part of it.
How free are you of such dominating insistence? _____

LOVE IS NOT IRRITABLE
An irritated person is easily upset or exasperated by petty annoyances. He or she "flares up" at the slightest provocation—and even at things not intended as provocations.
How free are you of such irritability? _____

LOVE IS NOT RESENTFUL
Resentment is indignation—often mingled with animosity—which persons feel when they believe themselves the victims of an affront or personal injury. A resentment can develop into a lifelong "grudge."
How free of resentment are you? _____

LOVE DOES NOT REJOICE AT WRONG, BUT REJOICES AT RIGHT
There is in all of us a tendency, never entirely conquered, to feel a malicious satisfaction and superiority when we hear of the blunders, inadequacies, or sins of someone else—and eagerly to pass on to others a report of this person's misfortune. This is rejoicing at wrong. Rejoicing in the right is to find happiness in the godliness of humankind and to experience joy in passing on to others a report of the good things people do.
How do you rate yourself on rejoicing, not at wrong, but in the right?
_____

By adding up your ratings on the above ten qualities, you will get an overall rating (on the basis of 100) of how effectively love governs your behavior toward all people. _____
(overall rating)

LIST OF
SOURCES

The quoted material on the following pages is taken from the sources listed.

7, 8. Frederick Speakman, *Pulpit Digest,* February 2, 1969, pp. 50-51.

12. Quoted in *Leaves of Gold,* rev. ed., edited by Clyde Francis Lytle (Williamsport, Pa.: The Coslett Publishing Co., 1958), p. 73.

14, 15. Neil Simon, *Sweet Charity,* act 1, scene 1. Used by permission.

17. Robert Louis Stevenson, as quoted in *The Minister's Manual,* 1966, p. 321.

21. Sydney Harris, "Strictly Personal," *The Chicago Daily News.* Reprinted by permission of Sydney J. Harris and Field Newspaper Syndicate.

26. John Powell, *Why Am I Afraid to Tell You Who I Am?* (Niles, Ill.: Argus Communications, 1969), p. 12.

27, 28. "The Velveteen Rabbit" in *Pulpit Digest,* November, 1971, p. 51.

33. Sydney Harris, "Strictly Personal," *The Chicago Daily News.* Reprinted by permission.

37, 38. Eileen Guder, *To Live in Love* (Grand Rapids: Zondervan Publishing House, 1967), p. 87. Copyright 1967 by Zondervan Publishing House and used by permission.

58. Sydney Harris, "Strictly Personal," *The Chicago Daily News.* Reprinted by permission.